D1472928

"Those strongest in the faith are those who've questioned their faith. In her bold new book, Sarah Cunningham embraces honesty, taking us deep into her evolving understanding of God and his world. Within her story she helps us rediscover a sincere wonder once again."

KARY OBERBRUNNER, pastor and author
of *The Fine Line*

* * *

"What an engaging book! Whether the idea of change excites or scares you, Sarah's moving and humorous accounts of her own life will inspire and challenge you to see any changes in your own life as opportunities to intentionally grow toward Eden."

MARY ALBERT DARLING, author of *The God of Intimacy and Action*

* * *

"I confess I wasn't initially excited to read a book about Jesus-gardening, but Sarah is funny ... and sharp ... and this book got me thinking more about spiritual transformation than any of the books I've read by old men in camel hair shirts. Turns out, following Jesus is as much about hugging my daughter and laughing at my failures as it is about self-discipline, accountability, and prayer. If you want to read a book about Christian spirituality in real life, then read this one."

DR. DAVID MCDONALD, coriolis: narrative,
Westwinds Community Church

* * *

"Sarah proves every person's story is unique. I wish every unique story was shared as honestly as hers."

JEFF SHINABARGER, founder of *PlywoodPeople.com*

Sarah Cunningham

PICKING DANDELIONS

A SEARCH FOR EDEN
AMONG LIFE'S WEEDS

ZONDERVAN.com/
AUTHORTRACKER
follow your favorite authors

We want to hear from you. Please send your comments about this book to us in care of zreview@zondervan.com. Thank you.

ZONDERVAN

Picking Dandelions
Copyright © 2010 by Sarah Raymond Cunningham

This title is also available as a Zondervan ebook. Visit www.zondervan.com/ebooks.

This title is also available in a Zondervan audio edition. Visit www.zondervan.fm.

Requests for information should be addressed to:

Zondervan, *Grand Rapids, Michigan 49530*

Library of Congress Cataloging-in-Publication Data

Cunningham, Sarah, 1978 –
    Picking dandelions : a search for Eden among life's weeds / Sarah Raymond Cunningham.
       p. cm.
    ISBN 978-0-310-29247-0 (softcover)
    1. Cunningham, Sarah Raymond, 1978 – 2. Christian biography—
United States. I. Title.
BR1725.C845A3 2010
277.3'082092 – dc22   2009040180

Scripture quotations are taken from the *New American Standard Bible*. Copyright © 1960, 1962, 1963, 1968, 1971, 1972, 1973, 1975, 1977, 1995 by The Lockman Foundation. Used by permission.

Any Internet addresses (websites, blogs, etc.) and telephone numbers printed in this book are offered as a resource. They are not intended in any way to be or imply an endorsement by Zondervan, nor does Zondervan vouch for the content of these sites and numbers for the life of this book.

Cover design: Curt Diepenhorst
Cover photography: agefotostock®/Hallmark Institute
Interior design: Beth Shagene

Printed in the United States of America

---

09 10 11 12 13 14 15 · 23 22 21 20 19 18 17 16 15 14 13 12 11 10 9 8 7 6 5 4 3 2 1

To Erik and Jill Weatherwax,
who are too gracious to ask others to change,
but have changed me by their example.
There are no words for what you mean to me.

CONTENTS

REMEMBERING EDEN

I was born post-Eden. This means, of course, that I came along *after* Adam and Eve's infamous fruit-pilfering and *after* the world had wandered many generations away from its original state of paradise.

As a child, I took in what was left of creation from the picture window of my family's duplex, which overlooked metropolitan Pittsburgh. It did not take me long, even at this age, to conclude that Pittsburgh was not Eden. For starters, all the residents, to the best of my knowledge, wore clothes.

A thousand feet below, at the base of the Allegheny foothills, lay the second piece of evidence that we were not in paradise: the less than illustrious Ohio River. Elthia, my childhood Sunday school teacher, had made it clear that Eden's river flowed through a land of gold, forking off into the legendary Tigris and the Euphrates. The Ohio, in comparison, was a mess — lined with plants and smokestacks and enormous metal cylindrical bins owned by the American Bridge Company. Not to mention the Ohio was bludgeoned by overstuffed barges and their gloomy, loud-mouthed air-horns, which I determined were not the vessels of paradise.

And although I couldn't always remember what God made on each of creation's seven days, I was fairly certain that on *no day* did God create a thick layer of smog to roll over Eden's skies like the kind I saw hanging above Pittsburgh. Animals choking to death from pollution probably would have put a damper on the whole "and it was good" theme God had going.

The Pittsburgh area, I was told, had *once* been a glory town in the height of the steel industry, but by the time I was born — long after Eden and also long after the golden years of Carnegie and J. P. Morgan—the town had slipped into an economic decline that would destroy half of the steel jobs that had once made her strong.

The land was not flourishing.

There was no gold.

This was not Eden.

When I was eight, we moved to Summerfield Township, a rural Michigan area that struck a tiny bit closer to Eden perhaps. Its landscape, at least, was filled with the same original garden content—animals, crops, and just a handful of people.

Summerfield was not Eden either, I surmised, as it had no discernable Tree of Life or Tree of the Knowledge of Good and Evil. It did at least have an abundance of oak, elm, maple, and walnut trees that lit up like three shades of fire in the fall and froze into a forest of crystal chandeliers in the winter. I didn't think God would've minded strolling with humans under these beautiful trees either.

Summerfield's friendly open farmland stretched as far as the eye could see, disrupted only if you traveled overhead via airplane where reminders of the less-natural world—the nuclear reactors of nearby Monroe—stood out from the landscape like rocket ships in a pop-up book about barnyard animals. At least once while I was attending Summerfield High School, adults wearing hazard gear converged onto our school, buzzing about the gymnasium with the sort of urgency we usually saw on television rather than on the streets in our town. These visitors, as it was later explained, were emergency personnel practicing their response to a nuclear disaster.

As it turns out, the first reactor prototype, called Fermi 1, had suffered a partial fuel meltdown back in 1966—nuclear meltdowns being yet another clue that perhaps Michigan was not paradise either.

Not to mention that the only famous person Monroe County produced seemed to be George Armstrong Custer, whose statue was erected at a prominent county intersection. Custer, I learned, graced the history books as an American general who graduated last in his class at West Point and went on to become most famous for a battle history calls "Custer's Last Stand." Even as a child, it did not seem especially desirable for your region's only hero to be someone well known for his *last* stand.

Summerfield, then, joined the ranks of fallen Pittsburgh, the two towns becoming only my first examples of an entire planet steeped in dysfunction and failing to live up to Eden. Perhaps it was these early observations, or life's shortcomings that I witnessed in the two decades that followed, that got me in the habit of thinking back to Eden so often.

When I say I think back to Eden, I don't mean I flip through a storybook, illustrated with Adam and Eve, whose strategically positioned leaves always provide exactly the right coverage. I mean that when surveying what is left of creation — the slumping economy and nuclear scares, the disease and societal breakdown — I fondly remember the *intentions* of Eden. I remember that God wanted humans to live in a setting that could be described as "good" and that the primary tasks he assigned to us were simply to care for our earth, to build families, and to flourish.

The funny thing is, in a world that is now light years away from the original garden, I think that is still what *we* want too.

Some days, it seems like my friends and I will do practically *anything* to recapture a little piece of Eden. We plant well-manicured gardens and keep nicely maintained homes; we build ambitious careers and foster pleasant workplace environments; we pursue education and recreation to their furthest extremes — all because we hope to create a little bit of paradise for ourselves and those we love. Of course, we may not formally connect our longings or efforts to Eden, or to God's intentions for our lives, but we are chasing ideals of goodness and contentment that may be rooted there just the same. I am like many people, I think, who believe deep down that there is something *more*, something *better*, something *beyond* our current experience ... something almost Edenic worth consciously chasing.

To some, that probably sounds mystical or transcendent in a way I don't mean it to. In actuality, I think the longing for Eden is one of the oldest and most normal yearnings humans experience.

True, some people's Eden yearnings do inspire them to go to extraordinary lengths to find goodness and purpose in life. But my spiritual road has been a much plainer one. It has not taken me to Italy or India or Indonesia to eat and pray and love like Elisabeth Gilbert. Nor has it taken me along a meandering liberal path through colorful California like the traveling mercies of Anne Lamott. Instead, I look for Eden from the starting point of my own life, alongside my family and friends in my own home state—the not-regarded-as-particularly-spiritual state of Michigan. And I find, to my great relief, that a person does not need to travel to exotic or cultured locations to grow toward God. In fact, I've begun to suspect that we don't have to go anywhere at all, because even after Eden disappeared geographically, God kept planting the intentions of Eden in each of us.

On the surface, of course, it doesn't seem quite as romantic to make your spiritual search among the farmers and blue-collar workers of small-town Michigan. But deep down maybe it's just as, or even more, transforming. After all, change isolated to an exotic location or a once-in-a-lifetime pilgrimage is easily lost to photo albums and nostalgia years later. But transformation centered at home changes us every day when we wake up and is still changing us every night when we lie down to sleep.

As I've lived and written about changes in my life, I've come to believe that the most powerful transformations are not distinctive, exclusive discoveries that separate one film writer's or one author's experience from the rest of humanity. They are, instead, pieces of personal tales that offer something universal. They are ordinary stories that point to the extraordinariness of Eden growing up among the everyday weeds of our lives.

PART I

Whether we like it or not, the post-Eden earth seems to present the perfect conditions for weeds like dandelions to thrive. Their bright tufts stick out of fields and lawns by the billions, highlighting the world yellow with their flower heads.

Because they are in ample supply, we might not blink to see a dandelion crushed under foot, or to see thousands of them mowed down by someone's John Deere. In fact, most of us don't appreciate a dandelion's strange beauty at all. They are a flower cherished only by the young, who pluck them with delight and present them with naïve pride to their mothers, thinking them a fitting token of their love. In the end, then, the dandelion's value is not determined by the quantity in which they grow, but by the insightful eye of the receiver.

1

I DID NOT GROPE MY WAY THROUGH DARKNESS TO RELIGION AS SOME do. Rather, my conversion played out simply, as if I were extending to God a dandelion: the life of a scrawny little kid pressed into his hand.

For the televised religious crowd who dominated the evangelical airwaves of my eighties childhood, faith came via sobbing supernatural breakthroughs or through studying complex doctrines. But for me, the daughter of a conservative Midwestern pastor, conversion passed almost unnoticed among other ordinary childhood moments. Somewhere between holding lightning bugs hostage in glass jars and sledding at mach speeds down Pennsylvania hillsides, I stumbled across the one referred to as God.

At that age I knew little about God and even less about life. I didn't know, for example, that with the casual gift of my life, I was pressing my entire future, at each age — eight and then fourteen and then twenty-five — into God's hands as well. I didn't know what sort of change would be required of me at each of these ages. And I didn't know that flaws in myself, in faith systems, and in life would push me to shed much-loved parts of myself, until I barely recognized my own spiritual reflection.

I couldn't have known the end result: that as dandelions give their white-feathered lives to the wind, the wind blows them — and us — to places where we grow in ways we never expected.

* * *

WILLOW TREES ARE SUPPOSED TO WEEP, BUT THE ONES IN OUR FRONT yard — swaying in the sunshine with their shaggy Beatles bowl cuts

—never persuaded me of their grief. Perhaps I overlooked their sadness because I was an early optimist, seeing the world through those vintage Windsor spectacles of John Lennon and my parents' generation.

One part hand-me-down hippies and two parts agricultured suburbans, we wanted to exercise our rights against the machine as much as any teenagers. Unfortunately, the only machines nearby were the kind that baled hay into neatly-bound squares or the kind that sucked milk from the local farmer's cows, so our rebellion never got much edgier than a high-school cafeteria boycott. We did, however, successfully lobby for more meatballs in the spaghetti in one moment of all-out anarchy.

However country our setting, my high-school classmates and I filtered our 1990s social climate through the ideals we gleaned from our 1960s-era parents. And so, we grew up beside the Michigan corn, desperately hoping the world would one day align with the images of brotherhood and peace in our senior class song, John Lennon's "Imagine."

But my own optimism was planted in soil closer to home than John Lennon's lyrics. I drew inspiration from my dad, who despite the Beatles-esque haircut in his late sixties high-school photo, was an unlikely revolutionary.

A Southern Baptist pastor who wears navy blue dress pants for a living, Dad insisted that the disheveled, weed-lined graveyard across the street from our house was the neighborhood's most attractive amenity. One day good Christians would rise from the dead, Dad pointed out, and we would have a coveted front row seat to the Second Coming. I imagined our family settled comfortably into yellow-and-green striped vinyl lawn chairs as a zombie-studded Macy's parade poured out from the cemetery gates. My brothers would hop up and down, eagerly announcing the moment when the marching band of corpses rounded the curve by our yard, throwing Tootsie Rolls and Laffy Taffy to curbside spectators like us.

The graveyard was not our property's only amenity. Four maple trees anchored each corner of our front yard, spaced evenly apart as if grown specifically to serve as bases for our kickball and baseball games, which were allowed up to eighteen million ghost runners (when you live that close to a graveyard, there is no shortage of pretend ghosts). The trees themselves, my brothers and I imagined, sprang from an underground sea of make-believe magma, modeled after the kind we saw in Dad's favorite science fiction movie, the original *Journey to the Center of the Earth*.

After my dad and Poppa framed the driveway with railroad ties, David and I, and even John who was quite a bit younger than us, responsibly informed all visitors that this sturdy maze of planks marked the only safe passage through a yard full of red-hot lava. To my mother's dismay, even as we rushed to church on Sunday mornings stuffed into flowered dresses and polo shirts, we would insist the only safe way to cross to the family's parking spot was by running, tipsily, one-foot-after-the-other along the railroad ties. We considered this route worth the extra time — even if it took twice or three times as long — lest the lava swallow us in tiny masses of burning flesh. We took our lava very seriously.

Perhaps our lakes of underground lava compensated for our parents' pathological overprotection, as we would not have been permitted to play within two thousand miles of anything resembling real lava. Ever. The only place we were permitted to ride our bikes, for example, was down a nearby dirt road that masqueraded as a real street but contained only two houses. This makeshift road, we learned, was named after Elmer, the man who owned our house before us. I genuinely assumed he was able to afford his own road due to his success in the kindergarten glue business.

During the rainy springs, Elmer's road became our own chocolate-colored sea, which provided us with sloppy handfuls of the chalky, sludgy mud that we used to cover the floor in our tree house. Not that our tree house was much of a house. More like a tree *plank* nailed onto our tree at an embarrassingly safe height. But later, when we needed more ways to swing above the lava, my grandfather added a rope swing with notches to climb and a round-seated swing on which to plant our feet when we Tarzaned out of the tree. We also added a rope ladder that could be hoisted up via pulley, to keep out any eight hundred pound midgets who couldn't climb the two-and-a-half feet to our safety-first tree-plank.

Our house seemed to *belong* on such an interesting strip of grave-side, lava-laden land, thanks to the mysterious secret passage (what less creative people might call an adjoining closet) that connected our bedrooms. To me, this seemed like a welcome escape route in case we ever needed to escape the always-looming, movie-esque "bad guys" who might appear without warning. The crawlspace behind the bathtub also seemed like a good potential hideout as it reminded me of the little compartment where the Jews hid in Corrie ten Boom's *Hiding Place*. Now, though, I realize that it's a standard plumbing feature every kidnapper worth their salt would know to check for hiding children.

All of life — our house, our yard, and the worlds of our imaginations — was a mystery like the Nancy Drew books I devoured. I was convinced the swirling woodwork on my bedroom door contained elaborate codes hidden from the untrained eye. There were also subtle secrets, overlooked by adults, in the rickety shed at the back of the graveyard and in the abandoned scraps of paper and pictures in our basement that made me wonder what sly, glue-manufacturing Elmer had been up to.

Unfortunately, our family's plot of land was swallowed up by hundreds of acres of surrounding farmland, whose nonmagical beans and non-fairy-tale-esque sheep — I believed — subtracted from our mystique.

The fields behind our home were filled with orderly rows of sweet-smelling corn in the summer, but were ironed flat by combines in the fall. In intervals between the two seasons, the country's comfort smells of dirt and growth were often overpowered by the potent cologne of manure. I was always a little embarrassed when friends came over after the fields were sprayed, as if our whole neighborhood had forgotten to swipe on the Speedstick that day.

We had good personal hygiene days too though.

Some days, when the rich summer heat hemmed the roads with black-eyed susans, Michigan lilies, and wild ginger, I suspected adjacent Ohio let out a low whistle at Michigan's beauty. I read, in fact, that John Steinbeck had once said Michigan was as handsome as a well-made woman. "It seemed to me that the earth was generous and outgoing here in the heartland, and, perhaps, its people took a cue from it."[*]

Steinbeck was right. We were rural, land-loving people who sheltered our one-flashing-traffic-light town from outsiders. Despite the somewhat lonely country existence, we were good and generous people. Our founders had, in a spirit of hope and celebration, named both the township and the school Summerfield. The name, which reflected the season when mayapples, goldenrod, and sunflowers bloomed most noticeably, served us well, providing an enchanting, almost Edenlike, backdrop for the scenes that played out in our homes and neighborhoods.

Summerfield's residents came in two varieties—one came straight from the earth and one was intent on building a life somewhere beyond farm country. The first set wore mud-colored Carharts that wouldn't show the stains of field work or the splattering from four-wheeling through the open countryside. These residents were always topped with practically rounded baseball hats, the baseball logo replaced by a John Deere brand, to prevent their three-season farmer's tan from requiring any aloe.

Because of where this set lived, back in the flat country plains miles from any paved road, our schools occasionally closed in midspring for mud days when dirt roads turned to sludgy muck that

_____

[*]John Steinbeck, *Travels with Charley: In Search of America* (New York: Penguin, 1980), 106.

could swallow buses whole. This provided hunters with more time to hunt, as mere rain couldn't prevent them from sloshing around the woods with private arsenals, spouting the words "up north" and "beer" as if they were passwords that unlocked a secret passage to paradise.

This set loved our downtown, an intentionally anti-metropolitan center we affectionately called "uptown." They took serious ownership over the rustic and historic town limits: a post office, a library, a pizza parlor, and a little comfort-food restaurant called Papa's Place where the decor transports diners to someone's cozy, flower-papered bedroom. Bars were the only things we had more than one of, and there was never much trouble finding a few people to take serious ownership of them, either.

Meanwhile, the second and usually younger set of folks talked about trading the small-town life for a more enlightened and trendy life beyond the corn and cows. This group intentionally swapped flannel shirts and overalls for a wardrobe inspired by *Seventeen* and *Cosmo*. They took their cues from Toledo, the bastion of civilization located twenty minutes south on US–23, where one could make pilgrimages to clothing meccas like Gap and American Eagle.

Truth be told, despite complaints about the dirt roads and manure, deep down most of these residents loved Summerfield just as much as the others and were equally grateful for such a safe place to grow up. And though remaining in Summerfield their whole lives didn't seem appealing, many found their way back, and I bet more will return in the future. Summerfield is a town that depends on its harvest—both of crops and of people.

Cars too, second to crops, were essential in this region. If you're a stranger to the Midwest, it's important to note that the car is to Michigan what the ocean is to California. Our region, just outside the illustrious Motor City, was populated with an inordinate number of mechanics, or at least those who deem themselves mechanics through a creative use of wire hangers and lengthy bouts of under-the-hood squinting. Here, bumper stickers that feature Calvin comic look-a-likes urinating on car logos tip off outsiders that in Monroe County, Ford vs. Chevy is a more heated debate than Republican vs. Democrat.

Most families in car country were polite, down-to-earth people whose youngest members still behaved as though they were actors on a sitcom set in small-town 1950s Americana. My more paranoid, Columbus, Ohio–reared parents excluded, some people left their homes unlocked and their car keys in the ignition. Besides a few who tipped the bottle too recklessly or who snubbed outsiders too willingly, the people of our region were conversationally nice and generally good-hearted—the type that would hook your car up to their backhoe and pull you out of the ditch before you could call a tow truck.

Most everyone believed in God, if not in full-fledged allegiance then at least in a sort of respectful nod to the Creator. Many were Christians the same way they were German or French and hence believed God deserved *at least* the same sort of polite acknowledgment as the person beside you in line at the bank.

I observed the town and its residents only partly as an insider because for much of my life, my family and I looked in as pseudo-outsiders who lived in the community but attended the Christian school. Fortunately, when I transferred to the public high school in ninth grade (the year after the Christian school closed), my family found camaraderie with local sports fans. My dad, especially, embraced the fans in gymnasium bleachers as easily as he embraced worshipers in a sanctuary, shaking hands, greeting people, and occasionally serving as stand-in pastor to the families of our fellow athletes.

As he interacted with the locals, or maybe just as he succumbed to country boredom, Dad, who wrote fantastical fiction in his spare time, transformed our rural surroundings into an epic world in his best unpublished work. He told my brothers and me, for instance, that an especially deep ditch that ran parallel to our street was what remained of the Panama Canal. He also claimed tiny white stones, which were prevalent in our yard, were fossilized dinosaur eggs that might hatch under the right conditions. I spent years trying to incubate them correctly.

These country neighborhoods were spacious and safe, different from the urban neighborhood outside of Pittsburgh where I had been born. The safety, my dad maintained, could be attributed both to God and to the Watch Cow—an aimless stray bovine that wandered near the fence line far from his herd. Dad claimed the Watch Cow was a specially trained lookout for lions, tigers, and bears. In response, my brothers and I rolled our eyes in an educated way, insisting that there were no lions, tigers, or bears in our area. Dad barely smiled while responding, "See what a good job the Watch Cow is doing?"

Near the cows were chickens that lived in tiny lean-tos, like their own Hooverville protests outside the farmer's home. Hundreds of look-a-like poultry were attached by some sort of wire to their A-frames, which led my dad to pronounce them fighting chickens. Dad said if they flew too far away from their training grounds, the elastic cord would snap them right back, which was part of an elaborate training regimen to build their stamina for the ring. It's not easy becoming a prize-fighting chicken.

Driving past the cows and chickens and the remains of the Panama Canal on the way to school, in the days when only my brother David and I were old enough for school, we would beg Dad to tell us stories about two siblings he named Daniel and Mary. As the stories unfolded, we would gape at Dad in disbelief, barely able to swallow that our dad somehow knew two children who were so similar to the two of us. Daniel and Mary, who were the same ages as us and who had our Hershey Syrup hair and eyes, were unfailingly reliable characters who heroically soared above all childhood evils. The stories always ended with a neatly wrapped-up moral, so much so that we almost expected the "The More You Know" logo to follow, along with a dashboard caption indicating that the public service announcement was sponsored by some place like the Will Rogers' Institute of White Plains, New York.

When Dad was not issuing second-grade parables, he would host a traveling game show on which David and I starred as the neatly-dressed contestants, sporting private school uniforms cleverly made from the world's ugliest discarded upholstery fabrics. Sometimes the game show questions asked normal-people trivia about the name of a Yankees' pitcher or the name of the first astronaut to walk on the moon, but more times than not, they were pieces of biblical trivia—the names of Noah's sons or Jesus' disciples—things that belonged to a million-piece spiritual jigsaw that we would slowly assemble in adulthood. Of course, Dad offered more than just regional folklore and collections of stories. If the townspeople found a pastor in Dad, then my brothers and I found Jesus himself in blue dress slacks.

Our family had less money than we had bills, an imbalance that mattered little in our minds if we noticed at all. Even as children, we knew that ours was a spiritual legacy. We were something of a spiritual Rockefeller family with a hefty inheritance of faith passed down from the previous generation. As next in line, my brothers and I were being intentionally groomed to manage the family's "wealth."

To this end, my brothers and I were raised on heaping doses of promises and belief—promises that good would prevail if we did what was right, and belief that if we followed in the way of Christ we would find peace and purpose, love and hope—essentially all the goodness of Eden.

Because God defied our sense of space and time, we knew that anything—using the broadest, most imaginative and childlike definition of *anything*—was possible with God. This birthed in us a solid confidence that, regardless of what life threw at us, if we looked to the hills where the psalmist says our help comes from, there would always, *always* be hope.

We developed a sense of invincibility, a knowledge that some part of us was virtually untouchable. The dysfunction of the world could swirl around us, targeting us with gossip, ill-will, downturns, and disappointments, but something deep inside of us was solid enough to remain standing. And we believed that life, in huge miraculous ways and in everyday ordinary ways, could triumph over death.

Seat-belted through daily leisurely drives in such an epic spiritual world, a simple Gerber-spoon-fed faith of promises and belief was perfectly sufficient for me. I did not require an aggressive faith since, at least early on, most of our lives played out in protective arenas designed by our parents, where it was easy to believe, unwaveringly, in the caring hand of God.

Of course, as our faith incubated within a controlled environment, outside reality was still a long way from Eden. But while I sensed, I think, that the unknown world held sadness and confusion for some, I didn't fully grasp that what lay beyond our yard might hurt people more than imaginary lava.

So as a child, my faith was just fine, thank you, swinging above danger to the safety of our tree-plank, breeze in my hair. Jesus made my hair fly back in the wind and that was enough for me.

2

HOW I "CAME TO KNOW JESUS," WHICH WAS THE PHRASE OF CHOICE
to describe conversions in the eighties, is a funny story—at least I
like to think that it might be funny if I could remember it. The fact
that I *can't* remember it, thanks to the hazy amnesia that sweeps away
most pre-five-year-old memories, underlines how little conversion
would've meant for me had I left it tucked in my Holly Hobby bed
sheets with Curious George and my very raggedy Raggedy Ann and
Andy back in 1982.

There *is* a legend about how I came to Jesus. My parents, the
hopelessly biased historians of the family, say that I decided to seek
out Jesus one night before bed. This is believable to me because, even
to this day, I often find myself thinking about matters of life and
death before I fall asleep at night. I think this may be one of God's
stealth strategies. The day saps our energy, and when the universe's
lights go out we're trapped alone, away from everything we can see
or worry about when the lights are on. Without bedtime we'd all be
much shallower people.

As a child, I *definitely* would've been more likely to summon God
at night when the nocturnal evils lurking in and around my room
came out to prey on what I was convinced was their favorite deli-
cacy: unnaturally skinny brunette children. At bedtime, fear charged
my room like a train entering its station right on schedule. The first
of the evils arrived promptly at 8:00 p.m., when the shiny brass
globes on the ends of my curtain rods grew eyeballs and began hunting for me. After slipping down to become nearly invisible under the
pile of blankets, moving under the radar of the curtain rod eyeballs,

I slipped off to dreamland. This was sometimes unfortunately no safer. There were two particularly horrifying dreams — one involving a "hag" (I had just learned the word somehow) who looked like the Wicked Witch of the West. In the dream, the hag fell from outer space through our ceiling and landed face down in the crack between the twin beds my brother and I slept in. What was scary, besides her hagginess, was that this green, wrinkled creature was somehow blinded from the fall.

Once she collected herself from her fall through the stratosphere, the hag stood up and unfurled her long, knobby green finger and wagged it menacingly at my brother and me.

"Who pushed these beds so close together?!" She snarled in the same sort of nasally anger typical of the Wicked Witch when she threatened, "I'll get you, my pretty, and your little dog too."

David and I, who were young but not stupid, did *not* raise our hands to incriminate ourselves.

"We're very sorry," David nearly groveled, as even in my dreams, David is much more humble and quick to apologize than I am. He is the peace-making middle child.

I, on the other hand, considered pointing out that it had been the hag's own choice to catapult herself through space without checking for an appropriate landing platform. Instead, I folded under her evil stare like a criminal breaking down under a heat lamp, and began offering excuses. "We have to push the beds close together so that our stuffed animals have a bigger stage for their nightly talent shows."

Stupid hags. Always thinking of themselves.

The other dream starred a camel — a cartoony cross between Joe Camel and our childhood rocking horse — who was sitting on the bench of our family's piano. He sloppily munched a peanut butter and jelly sandwich while talking with his mouth full.

Apparently camels have no better manners than hags.

The camel's voiceovers seemed to confirm that the rocking horse in our basement, which had unnecessarily demonic eyes for a children's toy, could also come alive and talk. Believing the demon-horse to be nocturnal, like other minions of Satan, I would bravely play in the basement during the day. But at night, I only allowed myself the occasional sprint down the stairs to retrieve a needed toy. I figured it would take the demon rocking horse at least a few minutes to unhitch itself from its springs.

Ironically, I remember these curiosities — the curtain rod eyeballs and evil camels — while my decision to follow Jesus is a blur. I won't lie. The fact that my conversion is not even a sticky-note on the hag's pea-colored face bothers me. But perhaps that's how humans are, even as children. We're branded by our fears, even the illogical ones, and easily diverted from our convictions when daylight and distraction knock on the window and let themselves in through the slits in the curtains.

As a child, the worst of my unknown fears were the ones that attached to religious imagery, like the possibility our house might catch on fire — which was my first fear of death and my first comparison for hell. Eventually my parents got one of those window decals that tell the emergency squad which rooms to focus on during a blaze. As if the Winnie the Pooh curtains weren't enough of a tip-off.

The fear of burning alive traced back to the day my dad stopped the car on the side of the road to let me witness the fire department as they tried to extinguish a burning building. I'm sure he hoped to instill in my mind the traits of a hero and the danger of fire, but an unintended lesson emerged. With my newfound horror of fire, I developed a dislike for the concept of hell. To this day, hell seems particularly unaccommodating.

My church didn't make things any easier. There was a poster on the wall in which small, shadowy, torture-faced people toppled off the edge of a cliff into a roaring lake of fire. So *of course* I "gave my life to Christ." First, on one reported occasion in my bedroom, and again every time I walked past the fiery-lake poster after that. Just in case.

As an adult, I once saw vacation Bible school kids raise their hands to indicate they wanted to follow Jesus. Their hands shot up as if they were being asked if they wanted to play dodgeball. Some of the kids raised their hands every night of Bible school. I remember thinking that some of them had no idea what they were doing. But then again, it might be our strange sense of lostness that makes salvation so necessary. We're so disoriented that we'll reach for something even in blindness. And sometimes what we reach for is real and right. And it reaches right back.

My salvation framework, which was loosely looped together like a paper-chain streamer made from sloppily glued colored strips, was not *all* about hell. There was also a trace of belief, however microscopic. Maybe if you piled it all up and squinted until your vision grew fuzzy, it amounted to about a mustard seed's worth, which is the amount Jesus said it takes to move a mountain. But I didn't know much about mustard seeds back then either.

Mine was not a fully comprehensive understanding of the belief statements they ask in church before baptisms. But I did believe there was a God. I believed God heard prayers. And I believed he had a son named Jesus. The existence of these two figures made up 99 percent of what I knew about faith. Maybe, apart from all the religious construction projects crowding them out, they still do.

I understood that there were good and evil in the world and, given the two sides and how Star Wars depicted them, I wanted to throw in with the forces of good. Naturally, I chose the side with light sabers, R2D2, and Chewbacca. I also felt a certain kindred relationship toward God, who I saw as more a powerful narrator than a Mother Goose, in that he provided the Bible storybook that sat next to the collection of nursery rhymes on my bookshelf.

I especially wore out the page about the prophet Elijah and the widow's oil never running out. This story was stunning to me because our family had oil. Real vegetable oil. Right in our house. We did not have a whale or a lion's den or an ark, but we had oil. The existence of household oil seemed to confirm the miracle's validity and its never-ending supply seemed to make God at least as cool as Willy Wonka, who came up with the everlasting gobstopper. I wanted to be on the side of the Being who could make things out of nothing, who could make good things endless. I still do.

I was also sorry in some gravely insufficient way. I believed that Jesus had paid a price for me. I imagined sitting on a shelf with a bright red clearance tag attached to my ear, like Corduroy the stuffed bear from the popular children's book. Then—what a coincidence!—*Jesus* comes along looking for a stuffed animal. I understood that Jesus didn't pay with money, but, for some reason, with blood. And I knew that blood, the kind that squirts out when you wreck your Big Wheel trying to drive down too many steps, didn't feel good or come easy. I felt bad that Jesus, or anyone besides my little brother for that matter, suffered on my account. So there was also a repentant, or at least empathetic, spirit somewhere inside of me.

Avoiding hell, befriending God and Jesus, and being purchased via a few drops of blood—that pretty much covered the scrawny beginnings of my faith. However scraggly and fledgling, though, I am not suggesting that I was insincere in my intention to search out God and follow him, jumping from footprint to footprint just as I did when I followed my dad in the snow.

In some ways, my conversion was probably as real and trusting as any decision I've ever made. While most interests from my childhood have come and gone, my allegiance to Jesus is still with me each new day. As a child, I believed, and my belief was a seed—early inklings of paradise planted just below the surface of my life.

3

HOWEVER MY BELIEFS BEGAN, I DEVELOPED BLIND-IN-BOTH-EYES faith. This was especially obvious in my interactions with my unnaturally short-lived pets.

When my first hamster lay motionless in his shavings one morning, I was not the least bit concerned. If Jesus could raise a smelly guy named Lazarus from the dead, then reanimating my handful of honey-colored fur known as Scooby would be a snap. Maybe it would even be accompanied by a catchy little Mary Poppins song. Without a trace of panic, I consulted with my mom about which prayer to say when raising a hamster from the dead. Oddly enough, apparently due to a publishing oversight, there was no such prayer in my tiny prayer book with a bluebird on the cover.

My mom says, to this day, that she couldn't bring herself to pray because she was afraid that—based on my unquestioned belief—Scooby might have shaken off his shavings and walked, prompting her to have a heart attack. Which is okay, I guess, because I would rather have had a mom than an invincible pet hamster. Although Scooby probably would've let me stay up later.

I took from this experience that expecting hamster resurrections was not the standard pet owner response. So I didn't attempt to raise Scooby or his descendants, Scooby 2 or Scooby 3, from the dead, nor did I attempt to raise my deceased goldfish, of which there were eventually ten or eleven sets named Titch and Grover. But when I discovered a pair of Goldies floating mopey-eyed and lopsided around their window-side bowl, I did open some great aunt's hand-me-down King James Bible—with the glossy copper-rimmed pages—and read some of the red letters. These words, which jumped off the page like color comics in the Sunday paper, seemed like a good funeral selection since they were the things that Jesus said. I also prayed for peace for my family as we mourned our loss and for my dad's willingness to take me to the pet store for one more set of fish—or for another Honey Bear (guinea pig), Peepers (parakeet), or Snowball (white mouse).

It's only when I write *all* their names that I feel like a serial killer.

So my young life was full of belief in and adoration for God—the Big God (the white-robed one in heaven, who I imagined looked like a glow-in-the-dark senior citizen version of Jesus), the Little God (the painted-face baby we unwrapped to set in the manger at Christmas time), and the Spirit God (who seemed like a ghosty sort who could slip under the door if you wouldn't let him in).

I liked salvation the way I liked Play-Doh and Colorforms and my brother's Transformers. I saw these and other "good things in life" as some special extension of salvation, as if God were the Romper Room lady looking through her mirror and choosing to call out my name. When he said *Sarah*, I knew that I was special, that I belonged, and that there were good things in store for me.

Unfortunately, Romper Room faith didn't transition well beyond childhood. As it turned out, God would not always deliver goodness in the form of free puppies and raises in allowance, but would sometimes spur his followers to personal growth and change that doesn't always feel like Eden.

Perhaps I should have picked up that life wasn't as whimsical as it seemed. When we were first browsing real estate, even our epic, lava-laden yard was not the fantasy land of later years. Instead, its backyard boasted a jungle of waist-high weeds, the legendary leader of which were the rhubarb plants that would not die despite Dad's relentless attempts to kill them. Even when he poured gasoline on them, the rhubarb kept right on growing as if thankful for being watered. As a result, Dave and I thought rhubarb was one of the toughest materials known to man. Rhubarb, then diamonds.

But as children in the Eden stages of life, our home and our yard and our lives came simply. And, to a great extent, so did our faith. We only had to present ourselves to God and watch for the steady stream of miracles we were sure would unfold.

4

THE FIRST "MIRACLE" I CAN REMEMBER INVOLVED MY GRANDPARENTS who lived in Columbus, Ohio—a location that seemed so far away to me it might as well have been Colombia. When my grandparents came to visit, it was my sole goal to get them to stay as long as possible. So during one visit, when my grandma announced they would be leaving in the morning, I defiantly told her I was going to pray for snow. Monstrous, street-closing snow.

The next morning it snowed. My grandparents played along with my miracle and told me they would have to spend one more day stranded, thanks to my prayers. However, Grandma told me in no uncertain terms that they would be leaving the next day no matter how much snow the angels in heaven riled up. "So don't get your hopes up," she warned.

When you are five, though, your hopes are always up. Being stubborn if nothing else, I prayed again. This time, I prayed that my grandparents' vehicle—a newish motor home—would break down. A sinister prayer.

The next morning we lined up on the porch to wave goodbye as my grandparents turned the key. I smiled smugly in anticipation. As if on a ridiculous marionette puppet string, the motor home whined and moaned in a supernatural struggle before choking to its death.

I actually cheered. God had changed something. My very own Red Sea was parting before me. My grandparents, however, did not appreciate my miracle. They kindly admonished me to go back to praying for weather mishaps, which did not result in such costly mechanic bills.

Later on I attended a Christian school—a nice private school where smiling adults had energy and faith, not just rules and paddles. One harvest day the weathermen reported a frost on the way. This was bad news for the local farm crowd and particularly for Bob, whose combine had broken down in the rush to harvest as many crops as possible before the frost arrived. News traveled fast, and before we knew it, our teacher was encouraging us to pray for Bob's farm machinery.

Of course, contrary to rational adult thinking, the combine started working and, by some reports, at the exact minute we prayed.

You say that engines sputter and catch every day—why bring God into it? I say that sometimes too. Actually, I say that most times. And when I don't say it, I think it. Combines *do* fail and recover, minus any supernatural intervention. But back then I *knew* God changed things.

After all, there were other instances: Josh's bike got stolen. It was a *really* nice bike, souped-up with flashy metallic rims and axle pegs that help especially coordinated riders do tricks. The kids in our class prayed fervently, as if our city was being penetrated by thieves who could strike any garage and steal any bike at any given moment. In our best imitation of the children of Israel sobbing to God from their Egyptian slavery, we cried to the Lord and we believed he heard us.

The bike was recovered the same day. Obviously, God didn't want those metallic rims slipping into the wrong hands.

A different time, someone broke into the school and stole a lot of equipment, including some expensive musical instruments. We prayed again, convinced that darkness was swelling against us in this string of burglaries. The same day, the bungling thieves tried to pawn one of the stolen guitars at the same shop where it had been repaired. The shop had its serial number on record and called the police, and lo and behold—our prayers captured a pair of criminals.

At that point, I was about ready to videotape *America's Most*

Wanted and start praying the country's biggest fugitives into jail. I figured we could put the FBI out of business by the end of the year.

Yet even in my Eden days, there were hopes and desires that didn't fall into place with my every "amen." Situations that didn't change. Things that weren't recovered. People who didn't get well. There were even people who died well before what the rest of us had deemed "their time." But weaving through all of life's good and bad was a fascinating number of prayers that seemed to find their way from the words of my heart out into the world where other people could see and feel them.

And so, in these days, I prayed for any number of ridiculous things that seemed to pan out. I prayed that the rain would hold off so my dad's softball games would not be cancelled and I could play with the other kids on the bleachers. I prayed that my parents would have another baby, even though they were already in their mid-thirties and seemed content with just me and David. During hunting season, I prayed that Terry—one of the guys in our church—would get a deer because I thought if he got one, he would come to church more often.

There were few rain cancellations during the years of my childhood, my parents had an unexpected boy five years after David's birth, and not long after I prayed, God seemed to wield his sense of humor in even the small things. Terry hit a deer with his car.

* * *

THE WORLD AROUND ME CHANGED ITS ATTIRE WITH EACH NEW season, like Mr. Rogers unlacing his shoes or buttoning on a new sweater with each new day. Stingy black walnut trees unclenched their prized nuts in the fall. Crabapples propelled their fruit onto cars as if hurled by a particularly violent squirrel holed up in their branches. The hawthorns removed their sparkling wreaths of tiny flowers before the winter snow came. And even the bean fields shaved down to stubble after the heat rolled out of town.

The countryside couldn't make up its mind—always approaching or leaving one of its four decisively different seasons. The old oaks and maples that anchored our yard transformed and evolved, shedding leaves and sprouting buds as if responding to the up and down zips of a divine orchestra conductor's wand. Even the willowy Beatle trees lost their trademark shags to baldness every winter. The world to which I awoke wore a new face each morning.

Change bloomed, grew, and died everywhere around us. Yet even skipping carelessly among the planet's changes, I had a particular talent for evading the obvious. It never occurred to me that I too might need to change.

5

LIFE WAS NOT ALL MIRACLES, HOWEVER. BY SECOND GRADE, I WAS locked in fierce theological debate.

During recess, a classmate in my Christian school—a chubby-cheeked beauty with enviously long hair that ran all the way to the end of her navy blue cardigan—told me, quite directly, that I was going to hell.

I stopped jump-roping and stared at her. "You know that, right? That you're going to hell?" she asked through a devilishly polite smile, as if she was going to get extra credit for personally escorting me to the flaming pit.

I stared at her blankly for a second, reviewing all that I had been taught about God and grace and how salvation is *free* before responding that I was *not* going to hell. After all, I pointed out, I was a *Christian* —why else would I be attending a *Christian* school?

"Maybe you should go tell the kids down the road that *they're* going to hell," I suggested, hoping that these kids—unrestrained by the peace of God that passes understanding and the fear of my father who passed punishments—might teach her a few manners the old-fashioned way.

But my tour guide to purgatory didn't budge.

"Yes, you *are* going to hell."

Then came her evidence:

"I *saw you* wearing sweatpants the day you came in to apply for our school. They were red with little pink hearts down the sides."

I responded with the only thing that came to me.

"So?!"

"Well," she continued, "*girls* can't wear pants. If they do, they go to hell." She reported this to me with the air of assumed knowledge one might use when observing that peanut butter goes *so* well with jelly and two slices of bread.

Perhaps she was used to weaker prey. Little did she know she was talking to the current champion of car Bible trivia.

"*That's* not in the Bible," I retorted, although I was only *pretty* sure on that particular point. I knew there was not "Thou Shalt Not Wear Sweatpants" in the Ten Commandments, but I couldn't guarantee they weren't nixed in the bazillions of laws about lobsters and linen and leprosy that came after the Ten Commandments. I did feel confident, however, that if Moses had anything against elastic waistbands, my dad and mom would have never let me waltz around in them.

My confidence wavering, the girl continued. She wasn't one to be distracted by hermeneutical inconveniences.

"It *is* in the Bible, actually."

Uh oh. Maybe it *was* tucked in there somewhere.

"You're *supposed* to be *kind* to God. And wearing pants is *not* being kind to God."

A lot of thoughts ran through my mind. For example, I thought about telling her that her insistence on continuing to breathe was also unkind to God, as she was not doing him any favors as his representative.

Fortunately, her brother—a boy whom I later rewarded with the title of my first boyfriend for his heroism—stepped in. "Leave her alone," he snapped at his sister.

She stuck out her tongue and began skipping away, no doubt to encourage more elementary sinners to fear the hands of an angry God before the bell rang. A couple of paces out, she turned to face her brother. "You're probably going to hell too, you know."

"I will, probably," he agreed. And then turning to me—the degenerate lover of red sweatpants with pink hearts—he sighed resolutely. "I'm not going to be a Christian when I grow up because I hate dress pants. I want to wear jeans."

6

As a child, I started with a three-bead understanding of salvation, informed by the cheesy but well-meaning WWJD bracelet equivalents of the eighties. That decade's bracelets consisted of a row of multicolored beads about the size of peas, whose colors—black, red, white, blue, green, and yellow—represented pieces of the basic salvation message. The black, red, and white beads were the focal point of the bracelet—the ones you would use if you wanted to explain salvation in a thirty-second commercial.

The black bead was the villain—the smoker's lung that showed how sin could blacken the lining of your soul. Fortunately, the red bead next to it represented the day when Jesus' blood ran down over the blackness in a timeless, regenerative antidote. Then followed the white bead, next in line, which stood for the new you that emerged, healthy and blemish-free like a newborn baby. All of this hefty theology hung on a bit of twine around your wrist for about twenty-five cents.

There were also blue, green, and yellow beads, but I never paid much attention to them. They were more like nonessential second-class beads, like optional fashion accessories I left in my closet most days. The blue bead, which symbolized baptism, was—I think—supposed to imply change. However, even my baptisms, which I have observed to be tremendously powerful as an adult, did not introduce change to me at this age. (No, baptisms is not a typo. I was baptized *twice*. I tell people the second one was a backup in case the first one didn't take.)

I racked up a second baptism when my pastor-dad changed from the Brethren to the Baptist denomination. When he made the switch, Dad decided to display his faith to the people in the Baptist congregation by being baptized a second time in the Baptist tradition. To me, it seemed kind of like he had just joined a new Baptist club and had decided to learn their secret Baptist handshake. You didn't have to do the handshake their way, of course, but it might be better if you did.

When Dad asked our family if anyone wanted to join him, I jumped at the chance. I was more than willing to get baptized every time I met a new person, if necessary, to make sure that everyone knew which side I was throwing in with.

I considered my first baptism the best one, however, because in the Brethren Church they dunk you three times in the names of the Father, the Son, and the Holy Spirit. *All* your bases are covered. The Baptists only do one lower-you-in-pull-you-out motion, which, if you do the math, only seemed to drive home one's allegiance to Jesus about 33 percent as much as the Brethren method. Besides, I wondered, what if an onlooker sneezed and missed the Baptist version? At least they'd still catch two dunks with the Brethren!

However the baptisms unfolded, I understood that baptism told other people you loved Jesus. What I didn't fully get was that the act of going into the water and coming back out of it was a symbol of my own death and resurrection to new life. I am sure my dad told me this and I may have even been able to repeat it back in a textbook sense, but since my old self was still eagerly awaiting kindergarten graduation, the metaphor didn't immediately stick.

The next nonessential bead in my jewelry line was the green one, which symbolized growth. I thought it meant that Jesus would literally help me grow tall, like some kind of supernatural vitamin, so that when my kindergarten teacher backed me up against the wall and drew a line on the giant ruler, my notch would always be two or three inches higher than the nonsaved kids. I could argue this theory worked for my brothers, whose green beads shot them past six feet tall, while *my* dud of a bead shorted out around five-foot-seven.

Even though I got my bead-bracelet spiel down to a compelling thirty-second infomercial, I still saw the bracelet as an evangelical tool for *others* who needed to change. People like Captain Hook and Darth Vader, and maybe my perpetually exasperated kindergarten teacher who used to grab me too tightly by the arm when I got excited about the bean-bag tic-tac-toe tourneys.

I picked up a little more information about change when returning home from school one day, back before we moved to Michigan. As the van pulled up, I saw a drunken man meandering along our uphill street, teetering left and right and resting his hand on the wobbly walls of stone that line some Pennsylvania hills neighborhoods. I raced into the house to report the incident.

"Dad, Dad!" I yelled. "There's a man out there and I think he might have rabies!" Rabies being the only disease I knew of that made things stagger about angrily and drool at the mouth.

Thankfully I have the good sort of dad, the type who at least pretends to consider the rabies scenario before setting you straight. "That man is sick," Dad confirmed, "but he got sick by drinking too much alcohol. He would have a better life if he changed."

I rolled my eyes incredulously. "Well, then why does the man *keep* drinking if it's making him sick?" I demanded. After all, that one rough night after I downed all my Flintstone vitamins was all *I* needed to kick *my* habit.

That question—why *don't* we change—was the first hint that conversion might require something of us that is beyond what we are willing or ready to do. It might be a process with ups and downs. It might be hard.

But that's where the yellow bead came in. All your hard work would be rewarded, not just in heaven, but in finding Eden in this life.

In the meantime, since heaven was a long way off, I focused on earning a different sort of reward: the affirmation of church people.

7

WIELDING A WITNESSING BRACELET WAS NOT MY ONLY MARK OF excellence. I also became *very good* at being the pastor's daughter —the way some kids get *very good* at soccer or the trombone.

During worship, I knew which drum beat to clap to and I knew when to belt out the lyrics in passionate allegiance with those around me and when to whisper the words softly so as to not interrupt the quiet, reflective atmosphere the music leader was attempting. I knew when to close my eyes and at exactly what angle to bow my head in order to give off the expected amount of reverence during corporate prayer. I knew when to open my eyes and when to nod and when to pick up my pen and use it to take "notes" to convey I was listening intently.

I had the churchy social graces in the bag as well. I knew when to lean into a boisterous hug from a suit-clad usher and I knew how to tilt my head to minimize the damage when little old ladies smeared me with lipstick. I shook hands and set up chairs and passed out cloth-covered teal hymnbooks—one every other seat.

I knew where to find anything you wanted: mops, Kool-Aid mix, or the tiny plastic communion cups that never hold enough grape juice. And I knew where everything belonged: what to do with used bulletins, where to stack excess chairs, and which families should receive the wrapped potluck leftovers that may or may not have been a blessing—depending on how much gravy was involved in any given recipe. If the church world had a Carmen San Diego game show equivalent, where kids ran all over the map putting things in the right place, I would've been the champion.

When I found myself in public prayer circles, I knew how to sound like I was praying to God. I found that the most successful prayers followed a basic recipe. Step one: Use a radio voice as if you are announcing a beauty pageant. Step two: Quote at least one Scripture, making sure to remind God of the reference—in case he wants to look it up later. And step three: Use a minimum of four flourishing "Heavenly Fathers," preferably pronounced with a mock Boston accent so that it comes out sounding more like "Heavenly Fahhh-dah." By default I learned to pray to impress, as if prayer was some sort of job interview where God was a good old boy in a suit and tie who would slap me on the back for delivering a joke that appealed to his upper-middle-class superiority.

I also took the adults in the circle to be kind of like *American Idol* judges. The more they said "amen" and "yes, Lord" while a person was praying, the better the prayer was.

I also really loved to worship. Sometimes it was because I thought, while singing, that something in my spirit sensed God's presence. But other times it was because the music leader used to pick people out of the crowd to sing a verse of a song before the entire congregation joined in on the chorus. Every time the worship leader did this, my friend Lindsey and I just about died from anxiety while waiting for him to call on us.

In my more focused moments of worship, I would sometimes picture God up in heaven at the top of a golden flight of stairs, looking down on us and smiling approvingly. Sadly, a man in our church told me my image was misleading because God was not actually "up" anywhere, but rather exists outside of time and space. After this, when I sang, I prayed that God would throw something from the sky at this guy to demonstrate how, by virtue of being God, he could sit on golden steps and listen to my singing whenever he wanted.

I also memorized verses. In fact, in school I was in a memory verse competition. In case you have never had the privilege of being a contestant in a memory verse competition, I should point out that it is exactly like it sounds. Whoever memorizes the most verses wins.

My strategy centered on locating and memorizing the easiest verses possible. I can't tell you how much knowing verses like "Jesus wept" (John 11:35), "Remember Lot's wife" (Luke 17:32), and "Job answered and said"—which is a quadruple score as it is reused four different times in the Bible—changed my life.

A little underhanded espionage always helped secure the win too. By employing the best spies and ensuring their loyalty with gobstoppers and stickers, I monitored how many verses my opponents had mastered so I could say at least *one* more than my competitors.

I am sure the adults who dreamed up the contest had noble intentions of planting God's Word in our hearts. But, I confess, we were mostly just seeking to slaughter our opponents.

And then, of course, after winning, we'd rub their faces in it . . . in the nicest, most Christian way possible.

If you'd like to polish my memory-verse trophy for me, I'd be happy to let you.

There were other ways to win in church circles too. The church's children's ministry also employed a reward system for doing things like attending church, which—being the pastor's kids—guaranteed my brother and me automatic gold medals. Once the church grew big enough to have two morning services, David and I became unbeatable, attending twice as many times as any other kid could manage. Ditto for bringing our Bible twice and knowing the weekly memory verse two times.

David and I earned enough points between us to earn plastic Jonah and the Whale action figures and a plastic Queen Esther action figure who fought many important battles alongside the Go-Bots and Godzilla in days to come. True, David's whale may have had size on its side, but man, did Queen Esther have a mean left hook.

These prizes—both the affirmation and the plastic action figures—made me feel like I was winning at the game of spirituality, chalking up enough points to secure my position among the leaders of the Christian pack. I was stunned, then, when I learned years later that in adult church there is no plastic prize trunk. Instead, the stickers and bubbles are replaced with a different sort of prize: acknowledgment, position, applause. And these prizes are doled out via completely different systems, such as the infamous church business meeting.

8

THIS TRIO OF WORDS—CHURCH, BUSINESS, AND MEETING—IS ODD to some, as churches aren't technically *in business*. And to others, the idea is repulsive since business and meetings and church sound about as enjoyable as having root canals and cataract surgery and several warts removed all on the same day.

But at age ten I was one of the rare procedural nerds who chose to attend every church business meeting I could—following along with the agenda, making little notes in the margins—while all the other kids, the normal kids, played Red Light Green Light in the fellowship hall.

In the beginning, I was not a participant in the business meeting, but an observer—a young Jane Goodall of the faith, studying adult humans in their natural church habitats. I was fascinated by every detail. All the first and second motions, all the "all in favors" who said "aye" and all the "all opposed" who usually said quite a bit more than "nay."

Every meeting, I sat in exactly the same place—blending my slender body into the woodwork of the pew until I was almost invisible—so that the adults would act naturally around me, rather than insisting I go back to play kickball or Simon Says with the others.

The only time I dared pipe up, in the early days, was at the beginning of the meeting when paperwork was passed out. And then I only spoke to volunteer. I liked to distribute the little stapled packets, in part to be perceived as helpful, but more so to ensure that I would get my own copy. As soon as I finished passing out papers to the adults, I would duck back into my pew and hunch over my copy with sinister attentiveness, reading every word of the minutes from the previous meeting—from the date centered at the top of the page to the motion to adjourn at the bottom.

I made a big deal of circling and underlining items of interest. For example, I found it interesting that the same deacon had made the motion to adjourn the last seven meetings! I circled his name and drew a bright blue asterisk next to it. This deacon, I decided, apparently did not relish the business meetings as I did; why was he always so anxious to end things? Perhaps *he* should be playing Red Light Green Light in the fellowship hall.

After a solid year of observations, I made the first breakthrough in my research. I discovered a technicality, much to my father's dismay and amusement. It seemed, as I read closely, that any member of the church was allowed to vote. *Any* member.

Possibilities began to form. I excused myself from the sanctuary —clearing my throat and feigning thirst—in order to go and check the membership list that sat on the desk in my dad's office. I scrolled alphabetically through the Clearys and Denharts and Phelpses to Raymond. Sure enough, there was my name, bright as the midday sun, beaming out from beneath my parents' names. Proof positive I had been inducted into membership the same day my parents had, back in 1986, when my dad took his post as pastor. I was *officially* a member.

I tucked away this evidence and returned to the sanctuary where I began voting almost immediately. I eased my way in, initially doing nothing more than following a script. When my dad, who moderated the meetings, said "all in favor," I softly added my "aye," trying to blend my voice in with the others so that no adult would notice.

Sometimes, when especially serious church women sat too close to me, I would sneak my "aye" out of the corner of my mouth or disguise it in a cough. I was able to slip under the radar this way—voting in hundreds of motions about everything from nursery protocol to chemical storage.

Over time the adults began to accept my participation—which is to say they probably never noticed it to begin with—and so I became braver. I began being more vocal, especially if a particularly important motion hit the floor, like when we were voting on whether the church should choose a "Western" theme or an "Insect" theme for Vacation Bible School. In life-or-death cases like these, where the success of the church was on the line, I began taking the liberty of announcing my "aye" quite loudly. After all, I couldn't let uninformed adults steer the church unknowingly, not realizing that insects were a billion times cooler than cowboys.

After a while, I even started seconding motions. I did not technically second motions based on whether I liked the proposal on the floor, but instead based on whether I liked the person who had made the first motion. I tried especially to second motions made by Clayton, who often gave me a piece of candy during morning church services. If Clayton noticed my allegiance, he did not let on, although he did sometimes slip me a whole handful of peppermints—perhaps to ensure my continued support.

I was also an avid supporter of Jack, of the prestigious Jack and Alma—the white-haired couple whom I had invited to my tenth birthday party on a whim. After all, they had given me money to buy a stuffed monkey, which wore a tiny, white and blue "Happy Birthday" T-shirt, and I was not above rewarding their gifts with political favors.

And I never passed up the chance to second Granny, who was the oldest lady I knew at the time, and who gave a vibrant, animated testimony about how blessed she was every single week. It could've been raining scud missiles and Granny would've publicly thanked God she could hear the explosions; after all, not *everyone* was blessed with a sense of hearing. It seemed wise to align myself with such a blessed individual in case there was ever some spillover blessing.

In all my seconding, I was especially pleased whenever it looked like my mom's friend Sharon, the church reporter, might be writing my name into the minutes. *That's Sarah with an "h."*

Once, in a business meeting, I even tried to oppose something. The opposition, which was briefly lived, was almost immediately squashed by my dad. He flashed me a very nondemocratic and stern look, which I had received many times before in various church services, from his place behind the little wood podium. It meant, in both cases, that I was talking when I was not supposed to be.

The issue that roused my opposition was a heated discussion over whether or not kids should be allowed to play in the church gymnasium when there was no scheduled adult supervision. I could not even believe such an issue had made it onto the agenda, as I could not imagine what kind of killjoys had the time to draft motions to ruin kids' fun.

I strongly believed that children had a God-given right to play dodgeball, which I remember explaining quite vehemently to the older gentleman sitting near me, who was kind enough to nod along as if he agreed with each point I counted out on my fingers.

"First of all," I announced, "playing in the gym is *fun*." Back then, as now, I ascribed to the philosophy that fun and church should seek each other out whenever possible. The older gentleman said he liked this logic.

"Second of all," I continued, "who are we kidding? Do we really want *all* the *kids* who usually play in the gym in *our* business meeting? Kids can be very obnoxious!" I reminded him, wisely.

The man gave me a cough drop to suck on and I wondered, for the moment before the menthol taste distracted me, if adults were really this generous with their candy and mints or if, perhaps, this was all a conspiracy to keep my mouth busy doing something other than talking.

The actual question I threw out for public discussion, which provoked my dad's eye-language, was this: "Why do we even *have* a gym if the kids aren't allowed to use it?" I asked this loudly, with a little bit of clever attitude, as if it were the closing argument of an open-and-shut court case, like I sometimes saw lawyers deliver on *Matlock* and *Murder She Wrote*.

The business meeting crowd, unfortunately, was not as easily convinced as the TV sitcom juries, and thus my comment generated less applause than I had anticipated. In fact, it was scary quiet. Even though my dad didn't say much, I could tell what he was thinking by his eyes. *You shouldn't have said that.*

I looked back, equally serious, conveying my own silent response, *Well, I shouldn't have to say it. It should be obvious!*

Gyms are for kids.

So kids should naturally be allowed to use them.

Case closed.

I motion we move this meeting along.

Even my eyes had a lot to say.

Since then, I've been the pained participant in more inflammatory church business meetings—meetings where people said vicious things about real breathing people, people who were sometimes even present in the room and who, in turn, said equally vicious things back.

But as a young child, the tensest meetings I witnessed were not escalated by personal attacks or gossip, but by something equally sinister: change.

During one business meeting, for example, we discussed an upcoming building expansion. Such building expansions could be a lot of fun, as practically everyone in the community is invited to pop over to the groundbreaking ceremony with a shovel or a little spade to dig up pieces of dirt around the new foundation. The end result is often a touching public statement that the community blesses the church's new effort. But before any building can be finalized, the church must survive the planning stage, which is often anything but unified. Consider, for example, the controversy of shingles.

We were going to have both the existing building—with its

sanctuary and classrooms—and the new addition shingled to match each other. This raised the question: Should we change the color of the shingles to a deep burgundy or a nice charcoal, or should we keep the shingles the same conservative speckled brown they had always been?

There were several ways this could've been decided.

By secret ballot.

By flipped coin—heads it's burgundy; tails it's brown.

But I learned rather quickly that matters as crucial as shingles cannot be left to the uneducated masses, nor can they be left to a game of chance. Each side must be championed until a white flag of surrender can be seen in the distance and there is a clear victor. Sometimes blood must be shed.

In this church building, there were a handful of progressives. These were brave, forward-thinking decorators who were ready to risk their reputations by throwing their support behind a speckled mauve and black shingle. They felt our rural neighbors would be especially appreciative of a tasteful mauve roof as they drove by in their station wagons and minivans and pickups.

But the larger camp was in no hurry to adopt some newfangled shingle design. In fact, to this set, change seemed like a preposterous and dangerous idea. To consider something new, some of them felt, would be to suggest that their first choice of shingles, the chocolate brown selected thirty years ago, had been a poor one.

And they did not hesitate to remind the others of several unarguable facts: Brown shingles had served the congregation well for many decades. We had never, ever had a problem with these reliable brown shingles; in fact these brown shingles were like time-tested friends—family members, even—who had seen us through many a literal storm.

By the time the majority laid out their case, I was convinced that all the Old Testament prophets, the twelve disciples, and all three members of the Trinity would've preferred brown shingles. Noah, I imagined, had likely used a nice brown shingle to complement the gopher wood on the ark. Clearly God himself probably liked a good, natural, tree-colored brown—or if he didn't, even God might've thought twice about commanding anything other than brown with so many brown shingle lobbyists on Earth.

It was clear, even to ten-year-old me, that a non-brown shingle would never be allowed to touch the church roof. If it came to it, elderly men would lie down in front of bulldozers and choir women would chain themselves to the eaves.

And so I was swayed to the brown side, to the side of God and good and, most important, to the victorious side. I put my new convictions to use as a campaign sloganist, developing cheery protest songs like, "Up with Brown, Vote Mauve Down," which I sang to the tune of "Three Blind Mice."

Brown shingles won by a landslide, and we breathed a sigh of relief. Once again we'd narrowly escaped change.

9

I HAVE A PHOTO OF ME AS A CHILD. TEN OR SO, BALANCING ON THE edge between the wonder of childhood and the structures of adulthood.

I'm sitting in a manicured garden, crouched naturally, the way children do who are not yet wondering if they are posing correctly, who are not yet measuring whether they are pretty enough in this moment to be photographed, and who are not yet worried about what others will say about their slightly crooked smile or that one stray hair that sticks straight up.

I am wearing yellow print shorts and a T-shirt with a yellow trimmed collar. My hair is a shiny honey brown, brightened not by highlights or glazes or expensive hair products, but by youth. And I'm wearing prescription glasses—pink plastic ones taped in the corner where my brother had cracked them because I tickled him too long without mercy.

In the picture, my tiny body is swallowed up by the tall natural grasses and white and purple sage of my grandmother's garden.

Grandma's garden was not dictated by suburban landscaping magazines. Although there was a standard rectangular flower bed framed by railroad ties in the back of her yard, the box was an ineffective restraint. Green enchantment flowed out and over it in a spreading sea of plants that turned the yard into the sort of paradise where little stone garden gnomes would have traveled across the country to live.

Grandfather trees—thin, wrinkled, and knotted—hunched near

umbrella trees that popped open their canopies, beckoning neighborhood kids to sit on benches beneath their branches.

Subtly tucked in this corner and by that rock, and in plenty of
places in between, there were pleasant sculptures—little stone frogs
and ceramic turtles and a peaceful St. Francis—who blended into
the yard as if they were born there, rather than standing out like the
unnaturally bright geese or fairies of some old women's yards.

A tiny pond with running water was a popular hot spot for local
toads and for my youngest brother John who liked to catch them.
The pond also boasted a school of sparkling golden fish, who froze
into the ice each winter, but to our amazement were still somehow
alive when the ice thawed each spring. Nearby, hummingbird feed-
ers attracted vibrating blurs that were assumed to be birds, though
their ruby wings flapped at such light speeds they seemed to have
no wings at all. Instead, they seemed to hover in space, propelled by
some sort of magic.

But the most enchanted section of the garden was a section of
exotic, specialty plants: Grandmother's award-winning, perennial
sucker garden.

When we were little, my brothers and I carefully placed our
little compressed-paper sucker sticks into the ground so that only the
soggy, teeth-mangled tops stuck out from the dirt. Then we would
sprinkle them with tin watering cans and leave them to germinate
overnight.

In just one night, our seeds bloomed colorful petal-wrappers and
sugary centers that waited, in neat rows, to be picked by our eager
fingers.

While indulging in the most recent crop of suckers, I wondered
if someone had put a half acre of Eden on a flatbed truck and hauled
it to Columbus to Grandma's yard, the way they sometimes move
historical houses to museum sites. It seemed to be the only place left
on Earth that had not completely deteriorated since creation.

The end of garden days was the end of childhood, the end of

worry-free Eden living when grandparents would live forever, when your parents were not the oldest generation and the ones who would grow old and die next, and when faith and life were simple and full of hope.

These were the days I would long for, but never completely recapture, in my adult wanderings to come. Instead, the older I got, the more life carried me far from Grandmother's garden, and even farther from that original garden of Eden.

PART II

When the dandelion plant blooms, it sprouts several flowers. Each of these flowers then produces a seed which is attached to a stem by fluffy white threads. Eventually, when a strong enough wind comes along, the seed bails into the air and parachutes down, floating to wherever the wind carries it.

The seed cannot grow unless it detaches itself from the original plant and braves unfamiliar soil.

1

As kids we sang "He's Got the Whole World in His Hands." "He," of course, referred to God, who was all-powerful, and I imagined—based on the song—could spin the world on his index finger like a Harlem Globetrotter spins a basketball.

But even though God kept the world spinning, it didn't mean that no harm could come to children like my brothers and me. This is why my parents chose schools that shared not only their belief system, but also their commitment to keeping us safe from the world's dysfunctions.

The school I transferred to in third grade met both qualifications. Its name was New Life—an obvious tribute to the transformation God inspired in his followers, though, again, the call to change did not necessarily jump out to me at the time. In addition to sharing the same faith, the school met my parents' basic safety requirements. Their recess monitors, for example, did near-perfect impressions of our mom telling us to stop flinging ourselves off the monkey bars or we'd break our necks.

This was a claim I heard often as a child: If kids persisted with certain behaviors—goofing around at the grocery store or walking a parking block like a balance beam—they would break their necks. Apparently the neck is the first thing to go in an eight-year-old. I never did actually see anyone break their neck though. Perhaps because in schools as orderly as the ones I was sent to, breaking your neck would have definitely been against the rules.

While, in theory, all schools are orderly, this one was particularly well organized. Hence I was the only eight-year-old in my neighborhood who had her own cubicle. Made from a two-and-a-half-foot square slab of table and fenced in on either side by particle board dividers, the function of such a cubicle, I think, was to protect students like me from anything that might distract us from our education.

The dividers were serious boundaries too, as I found out the day my teacher caught me reaching beyond my cubicle to accessorize the classroom skeleton with a Kleenex mini-skirt. That earned me a stern warning and the threat of a missed recess if I continued such defiance. Apparently, Kleenex skirts were strictly against skeleton dress code.

The school, like our church and parents, presented an orderly and safe Christian path to a blessed life. But even under the watchful eye of momlike recess monitors and within the confines of orderly cubicle arrangements, there were sometimes hiccups—tiny, seemingly inconsequential childhood breaks in the goodness that my parents and other Christian adults tried to create around us.

For example, our plaid uniformed jumpers, which were supposed to take the emphasis *off* of what we were wearing, could not completely shield us from the attention of the world's up-and-coming fashion critics. Instead, the bathroom where we changed for gym sometimes doubled as a runway, where unwilling models like myself had their clothing assessed by the unnaturally stylish children.

The worst fashion offense I remember committing involved a brand new white button-down shirt with a rounded collar.

My clothes had seemed perfectly acceptable to me when I pulled them on that morning. I was even a little bit proud of the starched "new" feel of the freshly-purchased shirt. But later that day I found out my pride was misplaced—which is something I've discovered to be true about four thousand times since.

"Look at her shirt!" one third-grade fashionista mock-whispered to her friend, pointing at me and snickering.

I looked down at my shirt, prepared for total humiliation, expecting to find I had missed a button while dressing. Or worse yet, an errant pen mark or a ravioli stain from lunch.

But the shirt was perfect—crisp, bright white, and buttoned correctly—just like it had been on the hanger in the department store.

My confusion continued as a second trendsetter fell into nodding agreement. "Check out the collar!" she managed to say through peals of uncontrollable laughter.

The uproar caused the rest of the nonstylish masses to pause their plaid jumper buttoning and turn toward me—some of them hungry for the little bit of drama we could squeak into such a well-supervised school, and some offering silent sympathy that I was about to be executed on the elementary school fashion guillotine.

"What's wrong with it?" I asked, my hands flying to feel the collar's stiff edges, to make sure it was not tucked in or sticking up in a way that warranted being socially ostracized for the rest of my life.

"The collar is *round*," the third-grade fashion critic explained through muffled laughter, as if a round collar was the funniest thing she'd seen in her entire life. As if rather than going to a comedy show or watching a funny movie, she would prefer to sit around and watch a round collar for hours.

"She looks like a Pilgrim!" her partner added, which caused both of them to laugh so hard that tiny, catty tears ran down their faces.

I stared at them blankly, unsure why it would be a bad thing to look like a Pilgrim. I mean, sure, they'd struggled to make it in the New World and would've probably gone under if not for Squanto and the natives, but the Pilgrims had done a lot of the dirty work in founding this country for the rest of us. Surely an occasional rounded collar in their honor was the least we could do to pay them tribute.

Apparently fashion overlooked their historical contributions, however, because the teasing continued.

"Which ship did you come in on?"

"Was it the Niña, the Pinta, or the Santa Maria?"

I considered pointing out that those were Columbus' ships and that Columbus was not, in fact, a Pilgrim. However, I didn't want to demonstrate too much expertise on the subject because I thought this might just confirm that I was in league with the ridiculously styled Pilgrims.

Instead, I made a mental note to throw away my buckled shoes.

2

EACH SCHOOL YEAR THAT FOLLOWED MOVED ME ONE STEP FURTHER away from imaginary lava and ghost-runner kickball. Over time, I began to suspect an unfortunate reality: Even the best efforts of my parents and their conservative peers could not guarantee absolute safety for me and the other children on Earth. This was confirmed to me the first time I was victimized by the malicious and wholly evil villain known only as "the school thief."

The school thief, as his notorious name implied, was guilty of stealing, which was of course a direct violation of one of the Ten Commandments. But even worse, the thief—to my absolute disgust—showed a complete lack of moral grounding by walking off with our most prized possessions: school money and pencil eraser dust.

At the time, I had more interest in school money than I did in American currency, perhaps because this Monopoly-like money, which featured pictures of the school's teachers, offered not only a cash value at the school store, but ongoing proof of what a high-achieving student and Christian I was. To cement my success in my classmates' minds, I liked to dump my money into a small pool in my cubicle on occasion and pretend to backstroke through it à la Scrooge McDuck.

My classmates and I mainly kept our stacks of school money in our pencil boxes, which we regarded as only slightly less secure than Brinks safes. This is why we were shocked when it started to disappear from such secure locations.

Unfortunately, the school thief did not stop with school money.

With sociopathic disregard for humanity, the thief moved onto stealing sentimental items, things we'd worked hard to make by hand, things that could not be easily replaced. Things like eraser dust.

In case you are unfamiliar with this valuable commodity, let me explain that pencil eraser dust is exactly what it sounds like. It is the shreds of rubber material left behind on the page when you use an eraser. But not just a little bit of pink shavings that you blow off the paper, you understand. Come now. *That* would be ridiculous. Ordinary pink shavings would hold little value. Regular pink eraser dust from a standard number two pencil was considered the cubic zirconia of the eraser dust continuum. You could buy caseloads of it on the Home Shopping Network for next to nothing.

The stuff that was *really* valuable came from rare eraser colors. Teal or lime green, for example, were particularly hot in third grade. And orange eraser dust? Don't get me started. I would've traded gold bars for orange eraser dust.

Another thing that made one's eraser dust collection valuable, of course, was quantity. The more you had, the wealthier you were regarded to be. Your wealth was judged by the size of the container needed to hold your eraser dust. A 35mm film canister of eraser dust was a sign of extreme poverty. People with that little applied for eraser dust welfare and the rest of us supported them by donating any unwanted, off-color eraser dust we were no longer using.

If you had a recipe box full of eraser dust, it secured you safely among the middle class. You might as well attach a two-car garage, a picket fence, and a dog to your cubicle. To really make it in the eraser dust world, though, you had to increase your supply to the point where you needed a separate pencil box, aka Brinks safe, just to store your eraser dust. That's when you knew you were living the dream.

Another thing that made the eraser dust industry so lucrative was the edginess involved. Eraser dust manufacturing was sort of like the illegal drug trade of the Christian elementary school. We were always getting in trouble for producing it, either because something occasionally went wrong in the manufacturing process and a pile of eraser dust got spilled all over the classroom floor or because we were abandoning all our school responsibilities in order to make more eraser dust. *I'll get to my math as soon as I grind this green eraser into a pile of shavings.* But of course, like with any good drug, I never did get to my math. Once you got hooked, nothing else mattered. On one occasion, the school staff tried to ban eraser dust, but this just forced us underground. A black market quickly surfaced.

All this explains, no doubt, why I was devastated, violated beyond repair, when my container of eraser dust was somehow penetrated by the school thief. I could not believe that a thief—who I envisioned as an adult convict, perhaps a prison escapee—had somehow perpetrated our *Christian* school! Was there nowhere in the world where a nine-year-old and her eraser dust were safe?!?

With a thief on the loose, no one could be trusted. Even best friends looked at each other with slight suspicion. It became protocol to avert your eyes if you saw someone making eraser dust, lest they think you were the school thief eyeing your next target.

After the initial shock of being robbed subsided, I joined other victims in forming a support group that tried daily to catch the school thief by setting brilliant traps.

Here was our basic strategy: We would mark our school money with some unique design that could *not* be replicated, perhaps a tiny four leaf clover inside of a heart *inside of a circle*, and then try to lure the thief into stealing it. (We did not use the more valuable eraser dust as bait, in case we were unable to recover it from police evidence.)

Our trap was of course pulled off with Oscar-worthy acting skills. One of our trained, award-winning actors would say loudly, "I'm going to put a ton of school money in my unlocked pencil box. Gee, I hope the school thief doesn't steal it . . . since it would be very easy to steal . . . since I am about to walk away . . . and no one will be paying attention whatsoever."

Once the money was lifted by the thief, the plan was to find some way to check everyone's school money to see who now possessed our cleverly tagged bills. Unfortunately, while we succeeded in getting our money stolen many times, we never succeeded in recovering any of it. I eventually began to suspect that these crimes were not the handiwork of hardened criminals, but perhaps an inside job. To this day, I'm still searching for the mole among us.

The school thief eventually got tired of lifting school money and eraser dust and other things started disappearing instead. Coats. Lunchboxes. Gym bags. A watch. A hat.

Even with God and a lot of protective adults watching, nothing was safe. Except, of course, my shirt with the rounded collar, which could be left hanging unprotected on a bathroom hook for hours without disappearing.

The school thief, who—be warned—could still be at large to this day, reinforced one thing: despite their best efforts, neither my teachers nor my parents could shield me from every possible harm that lay outside their reach. Beyond their safety-first treehouse and well-monitored monkey bars lay a world that was seemingly detached from the one I was raised in.

3

When the Christian school I had been attending closed its doors after eighth grade, my journey beyond childhood accelerated.

In the final weeks before the school closed, I listened intently to a chapel service focused on preparing us to go into the "world," which made me wonder exactly where we'd been living and attending school up until that point. Perhaps the Christian school was part of another planet in some other galaxy—a mere training ground for when we would be shot in pods, like Superman, to the *actual* Earth. The goal set before us, of course, was fitting for a superhero as well: to save the world, or at least, to point its inhabitants to the source of their salvation.

I had no idea what kind of torture was in store for me at the public school or in the surrounding *actual* world, but I fully expected—like the great saints of the ages—to be persecuted for my faith. I wondered, on some days, if I was the eccentric young David from the fields of Israel about to attend a school full of giants waiting to feed my bones to the birds.

As it turned out, the martyrdom did not begin immediately. Instead, I was pleasantly surprised when Lisa, who was unusually friendly and also unnaturally petite for a menacing giant, invited me to her table at freshman orientation. Lisa introduced me to the handful of girls surrounding her who smiled politely as one asked, as nonchalantly as she could, if I was "one of *those* kids from the Christian school."

I nodded, wondering if my Christlike glow had given me away.

They stared at me as if I were a lab specimen. Several of them,

I was sure, were contemplating cutting me open to examine what Christian-school-kid large intestines looked like.

I smiled up at them, awkwardly, from my place on the microscope's slide.

"Her dad is a pastor too," someone added. Helpfully. And a few more kids came over to look through the microscope.

For some reason we did not discuss what *their* fathers did for a living. It was not particularly relevant in that moment if someone's father was a plumber or a teacher, I guess. But at the word "pastor," a few eyebrows went up. I was hoping their reaction showed reverence, a hesitation to pick on someone whose father had an "in" with God, lest God wield a few lightning bolts in his daughter's defense. I knew very well, though, that this was not how it worked, and unfortunately, to my great disappointment, God never wasted as much as a light rain on the kid who referred to me strictly as "Holy Roller" all summer.

Fortunately, Holy Roller wasn't clever enough to catch on as a schoolwide nickname, so by the first day of school most kids were getting quite good at ignoring the fluorescent neon "She's a Pastor's Kid" sign I was sure flashed above my head.

I even got asked out on the first day of school. This was fortunate or unfortunate, depending on how you looked at it, as the guy asking me out inspired the first of several death threats that *almost* led to my martyrdom.

This guy — a talented football player from an athletic family — knew the school and surrounding community like I knew the church. When I, the naïve newcomer, fumbled with my locker during freshman orientation, he had it open within seconds. When I produced my class schedule, he hunted down other students who had the same classes and introduced me. He then followed these heroics with an unofficial, non-school-sponsored tour, laced with insider tips like how to get your change back from the snack machine *after* it dispensed your snack.

It was obvious, of course, that the football player, and everyone else for that matter, knew more about the school, the town, and just about everything outside of Sunday school than I did. They seemed to know more about alcohol, cigarettes, drugs, and sex. More about dancing, R-rated movies, music, and poker. They knew more about just about everything that many in the church crowd had worked so hard to protect their children from.

Of course, to say they knew more than I did was not an especially impressive accomplishment, nor did it make them particularly knowledgeable in the ways of the world. After all, I wasn't even allowed to watch *The Smurfs* when I was little. Hence I was not prepared when the football player sent word through the freshman grapevine that he wanted me to be his girlfriend.

Being asked out by a star athlete the first day of school? I could not have mapped out my first day more perfectly. All I had to do was say yes and with any luck, I'd be skyrocketed to popularity ... or at least some level of normalcy among the giants whose fathers were not pastors.

But when you're a manic fourteen-year-old whose pod has freshly landed in the "world," and the spiritual weight of the planet is on your shoulders, nothing is ever as simple as it should be. I was not sure it was wise to dive into a relationship with someone I barely knew on the first day of school.

Unsure of how to handle this scenario, I consulted my advisors, selected from the brightest minds in ninth grade.

"Sarah, you are so lucky," one girl told me. "You're getting all this attention because you're the new girl. Enjoy it. You won't be the new girl long."

"It would be good for you, as the new girl, to get in with someone who grew up here," another boy urged me with all the seriousness of a flood insurance salesman who saw a tsunami approaching in the distance.

I had my doubts, however. "What about his faith? I don't even know what he believes," I protested.

"Sarah, he's as Christian of a guy as you're gonna get," one of my basketball teammates assured me.

In the end, my advisors unanimously recommended I go out with the football player. I, of course, did what any teenager intent on saving the world does with unanimous advice. I ignored it.

After all, I didn't really know what the football player and I had in common, what he believed about God, or whether he — for example — had spent his entire childhood being corrupted by the evil Smurfs.

So, in the end, in a moment that was half conviction and half panic, I decided to give him the "same direction speech." You know, the I-don't-know-if-we're-going-in-the-same-direction speech. The one that normal people use when they are twenty-five years old and breaking up with someone they've been engaged to for three years.

In retrospect, at fourteen, the "just friends" speech would've been more appropriate . . . and more normal.

The football player took my response fairly well. "Well, let me know if you change your mind. I could be more Christian if you wanted me to be," he joked.

I sighed in relief, grateful for his sense of humor as I shuffled off to the locker room and then basketball practice.

* * *

MY RELIEF, HOWEVER, WAS SHORT-LIVED. JUST TWO HOURS AFTER explaining myself to the football player, I found myself in a reenactment of the rounded-collar scene from third grade. Only this time the antagonists were not interested in my Pilgrim-esque look as much as they were interested in beating the little rounded-collar lover out of me. And this scene did not take place in the locker room, but in the weight room where there are much more dangerous objects on hand to use to bash in someone's head.

It was after basketball practice and I was lifting weights. The phrase "weight lifting" would cause most people to picture someone bench-pressing a bar full of dumbbells. However, in my case, it sadly did not. During practice over the summer, the gym teacher had taken one look at my ninety-six-pound frame, which resembled the stick girl icon on the front of the bathroom door, and mandated that I would only be allowed to bench press the bar. No dumbbells whatsoever, lest I hurt myself.

Believe me, laying on the bench, huffing and puffing to force an empty bar into the air, was a slight barrier in getting anyone to take my toughness seriously. Perhaps this is why I seemed like easy prey to the girl intent on martyring me.

My assailant, as it turned out, *also* lifted weights. The main difference between us, however, was that when she lifted weights, it actually involved weights—multiple weights. Her muscles, though, were not the first thing I noticed.

The thing that jumped out at me, as she stomped across the weight room to where I was lifting, was her eyes. They were outlined with thick black eyeliner and heavy mascara, in a smoky Hollywood way that, along with her slick blond hair and muscles, made it appear that an angry Dallas Cowboys cheerleader was about rip the empty bar out of my hands and stab me with it repeatedly. Think American Gladiator or WWF chick vs. Winnie from *The Wonder Years*.

She wanted to talk to me about the football player, she announced.

"I heard you turned him down," she began, her eyebrows furrowing in perfectly manicured *v*'s over her Hollywood eyes.

I nodded, shoving my bar into the air with brute force.

Unfortunately, she lacked the good sense to tremble in fear.

A trail of expletives then spilled out of her mouth, as if she had been holding them all in like marshmallows in a Chubby Bunny contest and they finally came vomiting out in a total mess. I caught a few words I recognized—"Christian" and "snob"—and later translated her exclamations to mean she wanted to beat me up because I thought I was too good for people.

I continued lifting my bar—intimidatingly.

"Do you know how many girls would die to go out with him?" she asked, her finger and the body attached to it getting uncomfortably close to my face.

"Well, I'm not one of them," I told her in a tone I instantly regretted.

I wondered if the teachers would find me later, having starved to death after being unable to free myself from beneath the weights she would bury me under.

My antagonist fumed some more, insisting that I had made the whole school angry and that my classmates were waiting in a line that could stretch from there to Toledo to get their turn to fight me. She wrapped up the speech with a threat: If I hurt the football player, I would answer to her.

I wasn't sure if she was bluffing or if she really did speak for the entire Dallas Cowboys cheerleading squad and untold legions of other muscular blond girls with smoky eyes.

I later found out her army was much smaller than she made it out to be. But she did scowl at me really hard, like she almost *thought* about hitting me. And she raised her voice—loudly. It was enough to send a sufficient warning that I was beyond childhood and to foreshadow that the days to come would separate me even farther from the relative safety of home.

Somehow, by some miracle, I lived to see my sophomore year. And in the end, my martyrdom did not come in high school after all. Sadly, this also meant I never qualified for sainthood.

As I got older, I managed to evade angry blond hostiles, but I never did find the perfect formula for dating. I merely found a more appropriate scenario in which to use "the same direction" speech.

4

I HAVE YET TO EXPERIENCE AN ADOLESCENT PAIN THAT IS MORE pervasive than the awkward social ritual we call "dating."

The reason I know that dating is a universal pain, apart from my own experience, is that I am a high-school teacher. This means I routinely pick up school pictures that have been shredded—the eyes gouged out by push pins or the faces scribbled into satisfying oblivion—all because Ryan or Kelly or whomever, at age fourteen, signed the picture *luv u 4eva*, but did not, as it turned out, love past first semester.

Although I did eventually go on to date in high school, I emerged from these experiences relatively unscathed. My own experience with dating melodrama did not begin until I broke up with my first *serious* boyfriend. I met this boyfriend at the soda fountain, which sounds like a scene straight out of *Leave It to Beaver*, but actually took place in our bland college cafeteria.

He had a huge bruise on his face and I made the standard, smart-alecky wisecrack, questioning how the "other guy" looked.

He explained, sheepishly, that there was no other guy, unless you counted the ice skating rink whose floor had roughed him up a little.

Somewhere in the middle of his story, we fell madly in ... well, I would say love, but it was probably more delirious affection plus powerful need, the kind of feelings that make young people cling to each other like the life preservers you're convinced you desperately need to avoid drowning in four inches of water.

He soon became *the* boyfriend, the kind that inspired me to kiss in public and to make homemade presents and to lose enough grasp of reality to become part of one of the many syrupy couples I previously, and have since, despised. You know the kind. They fall apart at restaurants, unable to muster enough intelligence from their shared brain to decide whether to sit across from each other—for the eye contact—or next to each other—for holding hands. And they melt into pools of hormones, losing all functional language skills except for high-pitched baby voices and a limited ten word vocabulary that includes terms of endearment like "Sweetie-kins" and "Kissy-lips."

I am humiliated to admit, I was once a contributor to such crimes against humanity, being so enmeshed with the boyfriend that the tabloids, had they cared, would've taken pictures of us leaving biology class and blended our first names together like Brangelina or TomKat.

Despite the Valentiney cloud that surrounded us, the boyfriend and I were not the types who started out naming our future children on day three of our relationship. We did not have our wedding planned and had never considered whether our mutual morning toast would be made on raisin or wheat bread.

Mostly we flew on autopilot—the kind of autopilot where the pilot and the copilot are too busy making out while watching reruns of *Friends* to navigate well. In retrospect, this may not have been the best way to build a stable, lasting relationship.

Although I was obliviously happy at least half the time I was dating the boyfriend, I never considered whether we really wanted the same things in life, or whether either of us even knew what we wanted out of life as individuals.

Unfortunately, the older we got, the more apparent it became that we didn't have a clue—not together or apart. Neither of us were certain where we would live or if we would even stick with the careers we earned our degrees in, whether we wanted to settle down or roam the earth seeking adventure. As a result, we arrived at a dead end where we realized—with much agony—that if we ever did find our way to paradise, we would not be arriving hand in hand.

So we broke up—easy to say; hard to do.

Thankfully, the ex-boyfriend and I didn't cross all the way into hating each other. There were no dorm lounge cussing matches and no one's car was keyed, although there was certainly exasperation involved. Perhaps it was this civility that made me expect to be somewhat impervious—even oblivious—to the pain of ending a relationship.

As it turned out, I had underestimated pain's power to slice through my normal oblivion. Everyday routines like working at the college snack bar were disrupted by the ex-boyfriend's absence. Without him, there was no one to affirm how good I looked in the mandatory blue-and-white-striped dining services uniform, for example. Instead, I instantly devolved into the nerdy food worker in a striped shirt with no boyfriend.

Breakup pain perplexed me the same way the third-grade fashion critics and school thief did. I did not expect such annoyances to penetrate my life, and when they did, I often found myself unequipped to deal with them.

I was furious at whomever and whatever had encouraged me to dive headlong into love without first checking the depth of the pool. My list of suspects included Cupid, God, the president, my friends, and myself. Or maybe it was the advertisers who told me, over and over, that the mist of a particular kind of perfume was the exact recipe for two unnaturally beautiful, airbrushed people to fall in the sort of love where you throw back your heads in laughter in your shiny convertible for years of sunny days.

I took out my irritation on random representatives of culture. I'd mostly given up romance novels in junior high, minus a few I would borrow from my grandmother, of all people, when visiting on the weekends. But after the breakup, I angrily dragged the ones I had left to the used book store, thinking twice about even this, as if by donating them to future readers I would be setting them up for the same kind of amorous failure that plagued me.

I also swore off chick flicks, which I'd never been too fond of to begin with. I was never able to see the appeal of suspiciously stylish men with two hundred dollar haircuts and trendy leather loafers sending women dozens and dozens of enormous roses. What would be the point? For that price, why not plant a colossal rose garden outside her window?

We should all, I reasoned, be thinking a little more long term.

For most of the time after my breakup, I was mad at the forces of love and, like most of my screwups, not nearly mad enough at myself. So while my pain did produce some change, it was—at least initially—not so much deep personal change that moved me in a new direction. It was more a careless adopting of the path of least resistance.

Stop the pain, stop the pain, stop the pain.

Practically translated, that meant I was finished with dating, or at least finished until two years later when my husband tricked me into dating him by pretending we were just old college chums getting together for a casual cup of coffee.

Even back then, though, I guess I knew I wasn't swearing off men for life. I was more leaning toward short-term nun status, like Julie Andrews in *The Sound of Music*, who temporarily secluded herself in some sacred space until she got her head screwed on straight.

In the meantime, I ate a frightening amount of Kraft spiral macaroni alone in my apartment and watched way too many back-to-back showings of *Reality Bites* with my roommate, Amber. Much to my surprise, Winona Ryder and Ethan Hawke were of little assistance. Even though I liked their philosophy that "all we need is a couple of smokes, a cup of coffee, and a little bit of conversation, you and me and five bucks," it surprisingly was not the insight that righted my life. This, I guess, should not have been a surprise since I didn't smoke, rarely drank coffee and, in college, hardly ever had five dollars.

Instead, my moments of epiphany arrived via a slightly embarrassing source—*an advice book aimed at single women*. You know the type. They are filed away by the gazillion in the self-help section, all trying to outdo each other to win the cover-that-makes-the-most-readers-gag contest.

I would much rather say that something by Saint Augustine or C. S. Lewis, something profound and philosophical, ignited my intellectual revolution. But perhaps the combination of broken heart and mac and cheese made me susceptible to the pastel cover and flowery title-lettering I would normally sneer at.

After checking the area for potential eyewitnesses, I snuck open the self-help book and began browsing—not reading, mind you—a few pages here and there. In doing this, I stumbled upon the author's insistence that just as pearls come from the tear shed by an oyster, good things can come from pain.

This was Hallmark-cardy and cliché, but it was the exact little bit of cheesiness I needed, since any time I wasn't devoting to my *Reality Bites* therapy, I *was* looking for a way to turn my pain into something beautiful.

Despite its flowery letters, the book had a surprising amount of rational things to say. It claimed, for example, that while two broken people don't amount to a whole person, two whole people can complement each other. The lesson, of course, being that each of us should then try to be whole. Thinking back, I estimated that I was only approximately 56 percent whole when I was dating the boyfriend. No wonder things had ended so painfully between us.

Then the book reiterated the bit about pearls.

Women, it said, are often conditioned to believe that their lives do not *really* begin until they get married. Some women even save trunks of special items—good china and so forth—for the day they wed. Instead, they should enjoy eating from the china every day because—even apart from a man's validation—they are as deserving of nice things.

And then the book talked even more about pearls, and about how single years are years that are clear for the taking, years that can be poured into passions and adventures that aren't as practical after marriage. It talked about not focusing on finding a high-quality man, but on becoming the kind of person that a high-quality man would want to marry.

Then, of course, it was onto more hoopla about pearls. Apparently pearls are the perfect image to illustrate any point.

I considered loading my brother's BB gun with pearls and burning pearl-shaped holes through the book's pages.

But I also found little bits of relief. There were verses like "The Lord is near to the brokenhearted and saves those who are crushed in spirit" (Psalm 34:18). And this is what I wanted. I wanted God to be near. I wanted him to save me. I also wanted God to drop handwritten directions to Eden into my campus mailbox.

My prayers are often imperfect.

But somehow I find that God hears the prayers *I meant to pray*, the ones I should've been praying, which he drops in my lap after it becomes apparent that all I'm going to do is vent and snivel.

Somewhere, in the midst of all the reading and thinking and praying and pearls, I began changing. Not just in what Anthony deMello calls the "give me back my toys" way, either. It wasn't just that I wanted my boyfriend back, or even that I was shopping for an upgraded model. Instead, my search became much broader. I wasn't searching simply for a better way of dating, but discovering a better way of *living*.

That propelled me into the wind again, looking for a better spot to land. Unfortunately the path to my destination is often circular, as I frequently blow through life with no direction whatsoever.

PART III

The dandelion is a weed. But at least it can claim to be an *advanced* weed.

A single dandelion plant—which may grow multiple flower heads—can produce more than two thousand seeds per year.

Unfortunately, despite being so evolved, dandelions, like humans, do not always have a strategic growth plan. They simply grow where they blow, drifting off to wherever the wind or a gust of breath or the whack of a dog's tail takes them.

This is why dandelions sprout up in the strangest and worst of places, places they were never meant to be planted and where growth would seem nearly impossible—in cracks in sidewalks, beneath bleacher seats, or in the middle of a four-lane highway.

But wherever they land, good or bad, they grow.

1

LIKE MANY OF MY PEERS, I GREW WHEREVER THE WIND BLEW ME—IN Christian schools and charismatic ones, Baptist churches and Methodist colleges, homeless shelters and nondenominational mega-churches. Along the way, I found stretches of friendly soil, both in wide-open patches and in tiny bits of ground between life's rocks.

One of the places I lingered was Spring Arbor University, a Free Methodist college in Spring Arbor, Michigan. I, like most people, had never even heard of Spring Arbor—a rural town that doesn't earn a period-sized place marker on most maps of our state. I had also never heard of Free Methodists and had no idea whatsoever what they had been freed from. So I certainly didn't grow up dreaming of living in this college's rural apartments and scoring yet another set of cows as neighbors. Nevertheless, I still somehow ended up there by mistake.

In high school I struggled to get my locker open without the help of a football player, let alone to develop some sort of strategy for choosing a college. Every once in a while, however, I would sit down with several forests worth of college brochures and hastily fill out the corresponding stacks of "request more information" postcards. The plan was to acquire enough literature about each college so that someday—when I cared more—I could deduct important information like which campuses had the best guy-to-girl ratios and which cafeterias served the most chocolate cake.

While completing and returning these postcards, I apparently checked a box to sign up for a weekend visit at Spring Arbor. Or at least that is what the overly eager admissions representative—who

I suspected had been recruited from the school's cheerleading squad—told me over the phone when she called to arrange the details of my visit.

"Hi Sarah!" She immediately projected her voice through the phone with such chipperness that I half-expected her to begin chanting my name: *S-A-R-A-H! What's it spell?! Sarah!!*

"Hi."

"How's basketball season going?" She chatted away, as if we had known each other since diapers and had twenty-seven mutual friends.

"Um, pretty good." My replies were more cautious, like she might be an undercover telemarketer calling to announce I'd won a free magazine subscription, and then later mentioning I had to pay two hundred dollars to get it.

"Great!" She shook her pom-poms. "I was soooooo excited when I got your registration card for the Encounter Weekend!"

Here was the catch, I was pretty sure. I had never meant to sign up for such a weekend.

"Encounter Weekend?" I repeated.

"Yes! I'll finally get to meet you in person!"

I considered explaining there had been some sort of mistake, but didn't know if she'd hear me through all her high kicks and backflips. Perhaps this Encounter Weekend was more exciting than I thought. Perhaps they were giving out free cars or dates with hot male theologians-to-be.

"As you know, Encounter Weekend is the weekend where high school students come and tour the campus and stay in the dorms. I bet you can't wait to see what college life is like!"

You bet wrong, I thought to myself. But out loud I heard myself asking in a way that would earn me several stars for politeness on the children's church prize chart, "Um, when is that weekend again?"

She cheered out the date.

At this point, any normal person would have admitted they had made a mistake and graciously bowed out. I, however, could not bring myself to disappoint the telephone cheerleader I had apparently known all my life.

"Alright, I'll write that on my calendar," I promised, even though I did not have a pen and even if I had, it wouldn't have mattered, because I didn't keep a calendar.

"Excellent! See you there!" she yelled through her megaphone.

And I did see her there, later that winter, doing everything but cartwheels to convince me and other prospective students to apply to Spring Arbor. The gymnastics routine wasn't even necessary in my case, however. I genuinely liked Spring Arbor. I liked the people I met, I liked the feel of the campus, I even liked the food. With or without the cheerleader's antics, Spring Arbor didn't seem like a bad place to live the next four years of my life.

Granted, I wasn't drawn to Spring Arbor for the exciting night life. The competition for a fancy night on the town in Spring Arbor was between enjoying a tender Big Mac prepared by highly trained teenage chefs or raising a frosted mug of root beer at the only sit-down restaurant, the prestigious A&W. Outside of campus activities put on by a crackerjack student association staff (I have to say that because I was a part of it), students were stuck looking for less conventional things to do. Things like getting sick trying to inhale the twenty-one-scoop Dare to Be Great sundae at a nearby ice cream shop or going "chipping"—a more socially savvy nickname for dumpster diving—at a snack food company's local headquarters.

But it wasn't the ice cream headaches or free expired chips that lured me to or kept me at Spring Arbor. It was something less easy to quantify. Something spiritual that hangs in the air above chapel services or rests between students in late-night discussions.

I'm not sure how to explain that assessment, except to say I know that God sometimes had a special connection with a place—like walking around Eden or hovering over the Israelites' camp. I'm not saying I'm *positive* God lives at Spring Arbor in the exact same way he dwelled with Israel. But if he does, I think he probably has a condo somewhere in the tunnels they say lie beneath the college grounds. It is probably only accessible via a secret entrance too, perhaps something involving a secret lever on the fountain in the middle of campus. Or, at least it used to be a fountain, before the college oddly turned it into a garden after, rumor had it, the water stopped working. I guess they had to come up with *something*. A Christian college can't very well get rid of the secret entrance to God's underground condo.

The college chaplain, Ron Kopicko, had a saying he would often repeat during mission trips or spiritual life retreats: "There is nothing else I'd rather be doing and no group of people I'd rather be doing it with." Somehow that line described not just how I felt on those days—laying concrete for a church in Mexico over spring break or watching fellow students be baptized John the Baptist–style in the retreat center lake—but how I felt about just living at Spring Arbor during many routine days of my college career.

Though my theory about God's underground condo may not be widely held, the observation that Spring Arbor is a spiritually vibrant place is not something I cooked up alone. In fact, when I was in school, the Council of Christian Colleges and Universities conducted a student satisfaction survey where Spring Arbor's students expressed overwhelming agreement about the school's impact on their spiritual growth.

The survey results weren't especially surprising to those of us who lived on campus, as there was definitely a spiritual intensity about the place, not just among the faculty and staff, but among students. On any given night, for example, you could find a makeshift think tank of eighteen- to twenty-one-year-olds locked in spiritual and philosophical debate in Lowell, the dormitory where I lived my freshman year. There were no real qualifications for taking the theologian's chair and battling out opinions about social issues and humanitarian movements, although those who got an *A* in Chuck White's Gospels and Acts class were regarded as the more elite theological minds. And while I questioned whether developing philosophy between two-liters of Mountain Dew and back-to-back trips to Denny's on two hours of sleep was *always* a sound formula for arriving at truth, the learning and growth we experienced was surprisingly rich, and it linked our hearts in an ongoing search for God and his intentions for our world.

* * *

Spring Arbor was an appropriate backdrop for the stage of life I was in at the time, as at eighteen, my miracle-wielding childhood idealism had just entered its adolescence. It was perfect, perhaps, because despite being located in such a small, conservative town, Spring Arbor spent far more energy trying to convince its students to leave and explore the world than it did trying to get us to become permanent residents after graduation. This emphasis on "going" rather than "staying" seemed consistent with the way of Jesus, whose Great Commission had the exact same emphasis. It also fit with my own ideas, since I figured I might have to do a little traveling to carry out my plan to change the world.

The insistence that we get outside the property lines of "the Arbor" was what eventually led me to fall in love with the American city and later to pick up a minor in Urban Studies. And it also led to me becoming convinced that the church—though still not necessarily *me*—needed to change.

The first time it occurred to me, with any sincerity, that the church might need to change was during a service trip to Chicago. When you hear the words "service trip," you may think of "community service" completed to stay on some judge's good side and, if all goes well, to stay out of jail.

The good news is, this particular service trip had a different feel to it. For starters, no one went to avoid a prison sentence. In fact, no one went because of any official mandate, as the trip was entirely student planned and student run.

Once in Chicago, the student-made plans went brilliantly too, until the day we were charged with making Thanksgiving dinner for hundreds of homeless people. In retrospect, this is probably a task better left to people who have more cooking experience—and when I say *more* cooking experience, I mean *any* cooking experience. Someone over twenty years old may have come in handy, as none of us—despite great ACT scores and full college course loads—knew exactly how to make massive amounts of gravy from mysterious individually wrapped bouillon cubes.

About forty of us worked all morning trying to create a feast that would put Charlie Brown's Thanksgiving to shame. After we finished the prep work—a bunch of chopping and slicing that was somehow miraculously accomplished without a trip to the emergency room—we were assigned various roles in a Thanksgiving church service.

My friend Ryan and I were appointed to a team the organization vaguely called "crowd control," whose ambiguous goal, according to the stern lady who conducted our orientation, was basically not to let the homeless people start moshing or crowd-surfing when the pastor was talking.

About halfway through the service, a homeless couple excused themselves from their pew and approached Ryan and I with a seemingly simple request.

The request was presented by the man, a wiry skeleton of a guy, with a gaunt face and greasy, gray-streaked hair matted in place by a winter hat he had probably not taken off in weeks. He seemed to be the spokesperson for the twosome. "She has to go to the bathroom," he whispered to us in a raspy, cigarette-worn voice. His bony hand directed us to his wife (or girlfriend?) who was standing at his side, but did not speak.

The woman was a walking paradox—her skin pale like she had

never been out in the sun, yet simultaneously dry and leathery like she'd spent her whole life tanning. And that was just the beginning. The woman's eyes did not focus. She drooled a tiny bit at the mouth. And her expression hung lifelessly, barely responding to anything in her surroundings, giving us the impression that life had beaten the sanity and well-being out of her.

Ryan and I nodded and began leading the couple down the staircase, to the restrooms.

"Nah-uh-uh-uh." A cross-armed member of the organization met us three steps down. "No bathroom until after the service."

The man looked panicked. "She's got health problems," he said, delicately lowering his voice. "She *needs* to go *now*."

"Nope. Sorry. Sit through a service, get a meal. That's the agreement," the arm crosser responded. "No one goes anywhere until after the service."

The stern woman from orientation agreed. "It's policy. People try to use the bathroom just so they can try to sneak closer to the kitchen to steal food. Back to the service with you," she shooed them, as if they were pigeons.

"We'll go back as soon as she's through," the homeless man promised, apparently unoffended or at least too drained to muster an offense. "These kids can stay right with us to make sure we go right back."

Ryan and I cringed. A grown man was now negotiating for his wife's right to use the bathroom. It was not a pretty sight.

But the stern woman held her ground, directing them back to the service with an air of condescension that made the content of her heart sound about as good as the content of the stuff we were passing off as gravy.

The man's head hung, dejected, his eyes moving from his wife — who looked increasingly uncomfortable — to the pastor, who thirty minutes into his sermon, seemed to be getting his second wind — and back to his wife again.

Ryan and I looked at each other. Were we really going to stand there and enforce this ridiculousness? We decided to grab the homeless couple and make a run for the public restrooms at the fast-food restaurant across the street.

Unfortunately, when we arrived, somewhat winded from our escape from Stern Woman, the homeless man enlightened us to another unfortunate reality. "They don't let you use the bathrooms here."

"What?" We stared at him, confused.

"Let me correct myself. They don't let *us* use the bathrooms here," he said, with a sad, resigned sort of sarcasm.

And he was right. At home, of course, you could wander into any restaurant in the chain and use the facilities without anyone scrutinizing whether you had really purchased anything. But our covert get-the-woman-to-the-bathroom operation was sidelined when we saw the signs on the bathroom doors at this city location: "Paying customers may obtain token to unlock door at desk."

The area was apparently heavily trafficked with homeless people who used the restrooms to clean up from their nights on the streets. The only way the restaurant was able to prevent the homeless from sneaking in when employees weren't watching, and to avoid the extra maintenance necessary in cleaning up after some of them, was to go to a token system.

"Well, let's go get a token then," Ryan said.

"They'll take one look at us and that token will disappear." The man waved his hand in the air like a magician. "Paying customers only."

"Well then, you'll pay them," Ryan said, fishing in his pocket for money.

"Even if I pay them, they ain't giving us a token," the man insisted.

We decided the man was, unfortunately, right. So Ryan and I stepped up and paid for two combo meals, asked for bathroom tokens, and turned around—within sight of the fast food employees—and handed them to the couple.

When we got back to the church, our "crowd control" unit stood duty right behind the pew where the two homeless people who had lost their right to eat mashed potatoes and the nastiest gravy ever served at Thanksgiving sat, listening to the pastor talk about the love of Jesus and eating their combo meals.

The stern woman looked on from the back, annoyed, but silent.

Whenever I've thought back to that moment, and remembered her taking in our defiance with angry disappointment, I realize my actions may have been less that of the homeless vigilante and more those of an impulsive youth. Maybe her caution was warranted. Maybe leagues of crafty homeless people had feigned the need to pee in order to rob the organization of thousands of dollars worth of bouillon cubes. But something in me needed to respond in that moment because in this case, God's will didn't seem as hard to find as it was on other life occasions.

This time, we just kind of sensed deep down that the stern woman, and representatives of the church everywhere, needed to embrace the belief that Jesus wouldn't charge people to pee.

2

DURING THAT SAME TRIP TO CHICAGO, THE OTHER COLLEGE STUDENTS and I continued our service by painting and sorting clothes at the Olive Branch Mission. The Olive Branch was movie-esque — set in a former monastery still wearing its tribute to ancient days with its dark stained glass and stone columns. By then it had been remodeled to offer a residential substance abuse program and life skills training to people who needed more than one mediocre, college-kid-made Thanksgiving dinner.

The Olive Branch was also the place I would later live during two internships at nonprofit organizations in the inner city.

The first of my internships was at a warming shelter. A warming shelter is kind of like the heat lamp they put the entrees under in restaurants to keep them warm until the waitress takes the plates out to their tables. This sort of shelter doesn't attempt to engage anyone's problems; it just keeps the homeless warm until they can get to the next place they are going.

Warming shelters are particularly important in the Windy City, where temperatures routinely drop below zero and homeless people — at least a few of them — routinely freeze to death each year.

Chicago's air is so cold that when Oreon, the residence director at the Olive Branch, prompted the students who lived there to write our own verses to a blues song she strummed on her guitar, mine was about shivering at the bus stop.

Waiting at the bus stop (Imagine the bluesy ba-ba-ba-ba-bum)
Has taught me to pray. (ba-ba-ba-ba-bum)

God, have you seen the 49 bus?

Can you please, puhhhhlease send it my way???

I was, as you are probably gathering, crazy enough to debut my song to the people at the warming shelter, who were at first a bit skeptical of the preppy, white preacher kid's impromptu open mic night. But it won over at least one old guy named Paul, who went to work making me a handmade drum, and by the end of winter, we were selling out all three seats in the corner where we performed at the warming shelter.

It was while working and giving cheesy improv mini-concerts at the warming shelter that I discovered yet another way I wanted the church to change. This happened as a result of meeting the kind of people Spring Arbor wanted me to meet—people unlike those I lived among at home.

One of the people I talked to the most was Mr. God. While most of the homeless I met were more transient, Mr. God was one of the only people who was at the warming shelter the first day I arrived and was still there—slumped against the wall—the day I left.

This is how my first and most endearing conversation with Mr. God, an aged man in military fatigues, went.

"Hi, I'm Sarah." I thrust out my hand in the lily whitest, most Baptist way a person can.

He eyes me as if I am twelve and about to try to convince him to play freeze tag. He says nothing.

"And you are?" I prompt him.

"Mr. God."

"Mr. God?" I echo, confused about whether I am supposed to laugh at this joke or ask him how to spell it. "That's an unusual name," I decide to say, taking the safe and simultaneously cowardly approach. "Do you spell it just like it sounds?"

Mr. God does not spell it for me. Instead, there is more silence, and then he slowly stuffs one hand into his pocket and pulls out what he later refers to as his "real ID"—a piece of crumpled yellow paper that turns out to be the carbon copy of an intake form from a local hospital. On it, the name Mr. Godfrey has been shortened with the help of a black magic marker that is not magic enough to fully cover the "frey" that used to tail "God."

I eye the paper for a long time, feigning detailed interest as if it is a newspaper reporting that our country just declared involvement in an unexpected world war. It becomes apparent, during my stall, that Mr. God is not going to bail me out by advancing the conversation.

I turned to the only conversation piece nearby: Mr. God's duffel bag. The bag was weathered, with frazzled edges, a broken zipper, and enough loose threads that it could double as a mop if swept across the floor. It was also packed with thousands of coupons, ripped from Sunday newspaper advertisements and phone books and bound together with colored rubber bands.

"So, you've got a lot of papers there," I say, stupidly.

"Not papers," Mr. God clucks his tongue, suddenly recovering the urge to talk in order to correct me. "*Business receipts*, Sarah."

I nod, the presence of so many business receipts of course begging the next question out of my mouth. "What kind of business are you in?"

The answer? "A church–school–private–detective–agency–of–the–solar–system."

I swear. That is what he said. I couldn't help it. I had to ask. "So, um, what exactly is a church–school?"

"Sarah, Sarah, Sarah," he sighs as if I hadn't listened well enough the first time. "It's both a church and a school. In one. With students, of course. Paying students. It is a *business*, you know."

I nodded. "*And* a private detective agency?"

"That's right, Sarah. It operates out of a filling station. Not every place that looks like it sells gasoline really sells gasoline."

I ponder this for a minute, thinking this could possibly be true. I had been to more than one sketchy gas station in my life.

I never did ask about the solar system.

I did, however, make a habit of greeting Mr. God every day with my smiley hello, followed by a "How's business today?" which seemed to make him happy, as he would always sit up a little straighter and nod at me professionally. All he wanted someone to do—I think—was to acknowledge how important he was. And what could be more important that being *the* guy in charge of a church-school-private-detective-agency-of-the-solar-system?

Mr. God was not the only person I met in the warming shelter that I could not have met in Summerfield or Spring Arbor. There was also Ur, a lady who—panic-stricken—warned us not to enter the Harold Washington Library because our professor, who she clawed at, wildly, was leading us to our deaths in the gas chambers.

I realized of course that Ur had some sort of mental illness, though just in case, as we walked through the library, I kept my eye on the emergency exit.

Then there was Peaches, whom I met later on while on a mission trip in New York City. Peaches announced quite matter-of-factly that after she had begun living in a public park, the government had kidnapped her family as part of a conspiracy.

"How do you know they were kidnapped?" we asked.

"One day, after I'd been living out here for a while, I decided to go back and check on things at the house and—poof—they weren't living there anymore."

She said this as if it explained everything.

"The scary thing was, the government put totally different people there in their place. Like I wouldn't realize it wasn't my own family!" she said in outrage.

"How did you know it was the government?"

"That's just the thing," she whispered as she scanned the area for any eavesdroppers. "You can never know for sure. It's all part of the conspiracy."

These—and other conversations like them—were to some

degree comical, of course, but they were conversations shared with spent, depleted people whose lives were far from funny, and, I estimated, whose lives were far from Eden and what God had intended for humans to experience on this earth.

The thing that nagged my soul was knowing that some days the warming shelter was too full and we had to turn people away. The people would nod unsurprisingly when we told them to come back later, and they would shuffle away, down the snow-covered road and past the colossal empty churches that ten people attended once a week on Sundays when they made their weekly drive into the city from the suburbs.

My second Chicago internship was located in the Lawndale community, whose story is told by Wayne Gordon in the book *Real Hope in Chicago*.

In the late seventies, a group of Lawndale's student athletes convinced Wayne, who they referred to as "Coach," and his wife, Anne, to start a church. The first thing their fledgling church did was hold a meeting to brainstorm how they could help meet the needs of their challenged urban community. A lot of the ideas that arose were outside of the little group's reach. But one idea they were capable of carrying out immediately was the need for a safe place for residents to do laundry. So the group started there — not with a building full of pews and elaborate stained glass windows, but with an ordinary household washer and dryer set up in a storefront building.

This practice of expressing God's goodness through things as practical as laundry eventually evolved into the Lawndale Community Development Corporation, where I did my internship twenty years later. Today, in the neighborhood where Coach Gordon's church resides, you will see how the church's efforts have grown to include a health center; a residential substance abuse program; a counseling clinic; an after-school tutoring center; hip hop, art, and drama programs; a gymnasium and weight-lifting facility; a technology center; home restoration projects; apartment complexes; and a Lou Malnati's restaurant that offers a unique employment experience to those recovering from addictions.

After some time volunteering in the counseling center and after-school program at Lawndale, I set up a meeting with Coach Gordon to ask him one question that kept gnawing at my then twenty-one-year-old mind.

"I've noticed that Lawndale works with people from all different ethnic groups and social positions. Do you think it's possible for a suburban white church to accomplish the same thing? Could a suburban church lower its walls and welcome people from all over the community?"

I sat poised with pen against steno pad, as eager a note taker as I had ever been in those church business meetings. Coach Gordon allowed the silence to stretch out in thoughtfulness.

"I'm going to give you an extremely qualified yes," he said finally, trying not to discourage my idealism and yet predicting the result I envisioned was unlikely. "If that is really your hope," he advised, "get your lead pastor behind you or get out."

In the years to come, I ended up doing both, in that order—first, getting my lead pastor behind me, and then getting out.

* * *

I WAS STILL ON MY CHURCH-CHANGE KICK WHEN I GRADUATED FROM Spring Arbor and went to work at an inventive and imaginative non-denominational church in a nearby city. This church walked—no, sprinted—the slippery and sometimes sharp edge between religion and culture. They were proud of not being church "as usual," and this translated into weekend services that bordered on the unusual. There were makeshift beaches carted in via wheelbarrow, dozens of TVs tuned to static-only stations, and for one week a tattoo artist dotting a design into someone's shoulder *from the sanctuary stage.* All of this unfolded in the name of spiritual symbolism while singers sang and pastors preached and people prayed.

This was my sole definition of church for nearly six years.

During that time, I took on a variety of jobs in my quest to change the world—youth group leader, director of children's ministries, bulletin hander-outer (some were less world-changing than others). But the hat I wore most consistently, throughout all the rest of them, was that of overzealous social activist.

Eventually I managed to get my lead pastor behind me, as Coach Gordon had suggested. Whether he got behind me because he believed in my world-changing potential or because he got tired of me complaining about all the opportunities we were missing to change the world, I've never been sure. But I didn't really care why, since he created a new position for me, which the church titled Director of Outreach, only—I think—because "overzealous social activist" didn't sound as good on business cards.

My job was to oversee our church's efforts outside of our building's four walls—locally, regionally, and internationally. With a job description that broad, there was generous space for creating a work week I could love. Before long, I was eating, drinking, and breathing church and having the time of my life doing it.

I raced to work every day and stayed many late nights with volunteers as we happily planned service projects for our church's small groups, community improvement days in Detroit and Chicago, and mission trips to Mexico or Canada. Our goal was to be present at every local community event, even if it was doing something as small as handing out flags at the Memorial Day fireworks or offering free oil changes and minor car repairs to single mothers. I fell asleep at night happy to be alive, barely able to believe that this was *my job*, that I was *getting paid* to do inspiring things like talk to missionaries about the foreign cultures they lived in or help sponsor Christmas for the children in a South African AIDS orphanage where a church member was working.

As time went on and ideas began to click in our heads, the volunteers and I began going in less conventional directions. Rather than recruit church attendees to help us put on individual outreach events, we decided our work would have more lasting impact if we helped them look for ways to express God's goodness to those in need regardless of which ministry area they worked in or where in the world they might end up living. It was a difference between getting church attendees to "do" outreach and encouraging church attendees to "live" as the church.

And so, along these lines, we staged a prayer night, for example, which equipped each room in the church with a station where people could pray for the inhabitants of a different continent. Facts about world issues—poverty, health, and racial violence—were printed on cards available to those who came to pray. The sanctuary hosted a huge floor map of our city, where church members could stand or sit on different landmarks to pray for the residents of our town. Around that there were smaller, individual stations—tables full of local phone books, newspapers, and lists of schools and city officials —that people were encouraged to reflect and pray over.

By far my favorite part of the job, however, was hosting training events aimed at helping locals get to know those unlike themselves, much like Spring Arbor and my experiences in Chicago had done for me. One night, we sent church members to all the various restaurants around town to buy ten dollars' worth of food at each establishment. When they returned, we talked for hours about the things they observed in the different areas of our community while sampling the Chinese, Mexican, American, and soul food smorgasbord that reflected the diverse taste buds of our city.

Another day, we split up and went to local Laundromats—in the more underprivileged parts of our town—just to do something as simple as fold towels and T-shirts with residents on another side of the city. We observed firsthand how the workload of a single mother who has to lug three children and a shopping cart full of baby clothes several blocks to a Laundromat might differ from the chores of a suburban housewife who tosses dirty clothes into a main floor laundry room. Or we noted how an elderly man had to skip filling a prescription in order to spare enough quarters to wash his meager wardrobe of sweatshirts and work pants.

We rode the city buses to various locations around town, to see what people who depended on public transportation had to pay attention to every day. Wheelchairs, we found, barely fit through the aisles on some buses. Bus routes didn't run to churches on weekends. The transportation system didn't operate late enough at night to keep a working class father from having to regularly walk home in the snow.

Along the way, in this job as overzealous social activist, there were shining moments like our congregation's generous participation in Angel Tree, the program that ensures that the children of those who are incarcerated get Christmas presents. After buying presents for all the children on the list for our city, which is the hometown of the state prison, we learned that more than a hundred children in Detroit were not going to be sponsored by any organization. There simply weren't enough donors in that area to go around. When I told our congregation what we had heard about the unclaimed kids, not only did hundreds of additional gifts pour in, but that same Sunday, a couple stepped forward and volunteered to pay for *all* the postage to mail the gifts out in time for Christmas.

One Sunday, in tandem with the associate pastor, I was given the chance to offer a speech that I called "Excellence of Heart." During my time on stage, I told a story about a girl I met at a homeless shelter. The girl had been routinely locked outside on a tiny, second-floor balcony, without food or restroom facilities, whenever her addicted mother went out to party or restock her supply of coke. The neighbor child, she had told me, used to try to throw Ziploc bags with sandwiches in them up to her while she was stranded outside her home waiting for her mom to return and remember her. Her situation was eventually reported to social services, and the foster mom who took her in even brought her to church. But, unfortunately, the little girl was treated like an outcast by a Sunday school friend's mother who saw her as coming from "bad stock," which sent the girl an unfortunate message about God's people and what they thought of people like her, who lived on society's margins.

As the congregation listened, they naturally assumed that this story was about a girl I had encountered in a large metropolitan area during my travels to places like Chicago or New York. So when I revealed that she lived right there in our city, less than three miles from our building, I felt like I was watching the church's collective heart break all at once—as waves of recognition spread over the listeners' faces. I remember looking out at them, my heart heavy with seriousness, and saying, "I don't know about you, but I'm not okay with that being the experience of people in this town."

I asked them to join me in being dissatisfied with people living that close to our doors encountering that kind of judgment, rather than God's intended love, in the local church. And when I finished my spiel, after the three services ended, more than two hundred people had signed index cards volunteering to help with our upcoming outreach events.

I was on top of the world.

So there were good, good moments—moments where church was everything I hoped it could be. But there were, of course, moments that did not always go as I had hoped either, moments where it was tricky to be twenty-three and navigating a movement fueled by dissatisfaction with how things are.

Not to mention the church had other legitimately good things going on too, other ministry areas to champion, and other accomplishments that generated regional interest in how we did worship services, for example. As a result, outreach didn't always fall where I had dreamed it could on the priority list. And the pace at which my team was able to implement ideas was sometimes much slower and harder won than I anticipated.

Over time I became unsure, at the rate we were going, that we'd be able to change the whole world in my lifetime. It seemed, on the bad days, as though we might have to settle for transforming just a couple continents.

And so there were days when I complained loudly, like the day when the church decided to offer the sermon notes in thirty-dollar leather journals emblazoned with our church logo—a stylish, but pricey, accessory I felt outpaced the budgets of some in our mainly blue-collar surroundings. I tempered my rants about economic disparity and other socio-spiritual issues with *just barely* enough solutions to *just barely* keep my job off the chopping block. And along the way, I attempted to equalize many facets of church participation that never succeeded and a few that did—starting with journal ownership.

I was both loved and tolerated for my efforts, depending on the day or the people involved or the immaturity behind my antagonism. Thus, I spent a lot of time testing the winds. Blowing back and forth between idealism and reality, I spun clockwise and counterclockwise, disoriented, like a weather vane trying to both accommodate and resist the world's hurricane gales.

As much as I loved the world and faith as it was, I longed for the world and faith as I believed it *could be*. And like many aspiring world-changers, I thought I could somehow be a bridge between the two.

Some days I was. And people crossed me to the hope of a better way. Some days, though, I just got walked on. And still other days I became an unreliable structure, crumbling into the water beneath me and stranding those who were with me between two lands.

In the end, we changed less of the world than I had hoped, not even solving the problems of the continent we were on, let alone making a dent in the others. Instead, a lot of unanticipated change was thrust upon us, as the church where I worked ended up in major transition.

There was also transition in my life. I got married and eventually ended up following Coach Gordon's second piece of advice: I got out of suburbia. My husband and I moved to the south side of our city, among a more diverse population, and went to work in a school serving a diverse mix of students who were often unsuccessful in the local public schools.

All of this, of course, became another lesson on change because, as much as I resisted the winds at the time, the direction it took me often ended up being for the best. I was disappointed that things at the church had not worked out more closely with my expectations though. And I was saddened to no longer have any formal opportunities to encourage church people to reach out to those who were marginalized by society. I decided one of the only things I could do, completely on my own, was start a web resource for churches who wanted to build relationships with diverse people groups.

One day, while writing a resource about the church's response to depression, I interviewed Ben DeVries, the author of *A Delicate Fade*. Ben was a total stranger, but the conversation flowed easily—in part because being raised as the son of a missionary led him to make many of the same observations I did about growing up in the church.

A few days later, unbeknownst to me, Ben directed his publisher to some of the articles I had posted. The result, my first book, *Dear Church: Letters from a Disillusioned Generation*, gave me a far larger audience than I had ever had at that one local church. And if it wasn't for that book, I never would've met some of the inspiring people I've run into and encouraged along the path of outreach while touring and speaking around the country.

Apparently, even when you do everything in your power to propel yourself in a certain direction, the wind doesn't always cooperate with your deepest desires. Sometimes it just moves the way it wants to. And then one day, when you're quiet, and you accept where the gust is taking you, you gradually learn to trust that the force behind the wind knows best.

PART IV

Even the most free-flying of dandelions cannot always zip freely through the air, swishing about at its every whim. Rather, the seed finds objects in its path that it cannot easily careen around or through and the only remaining choice is to smack right into them. Unfortunately, fences or walls or other permanent structures are not ideal soil for growth. Although it is possible to continue growing in a carefully found crevice or crack, the dandelion must learn to really dig in if it wants to survive.

1

While working at this church, my generation and I hit our first major obstacle. Like a seed crashing into a wall, we could drift no further. Our only choice was to drop down, dig deep, and try to grow.

Compared to the sacrifices of young people in World War II or Vietnam, my peers and I enjoyed a historical stretch of garden living. Duty was not thrust upon us at the scale it was heaved upon previous generations, so for much of adolescence, we had the luxury of blowing aimlessly about our world while we tried to figure out where to go and what to do with our lives.

The media, observing our slow migration into adulthood, even made up little nicknames for us like "kiddults" and "adultolescents."

Yeah well, sticks and stones, media. Sticks and stones.

The day that halted my generation's leisurely flight, I reported to work as usual just as the tragedy up the coastline hit the news.

"Did you hear that a plane just hit the World Trade Center Tower in New York?" the church receptionist asked me as I passed her desk on the way back to my office.

That's weird, I remember thinking. Why is the church receptionist suddenly playing anchor woman? She's never passed on a headline before.

But this alone was not enough to jar my oblivion. The news was still calling the crash an accident and thus, my reaction was somewhat shrugging disregard, mustering only momentary empathy for the family of whatever pilot had manned what I expected was a twin-engine plane crash.

This, I'm afraid, is the way I hear—or rather *don't hear*—the daily news. I consider whatever trauma or tragedy is reported for just a minute before letting my music or my shopping list sweep it away.

It wasn't until the plane was identified as an airliner that my heart joined my head in listening. And it wasn't until a second plane crashed and the FAA grounded all planes that I began to realize how my generation's conception of our world was crashing as well.

While newscasters warned the general public *not* to show up in the Big Apple to offer unqualified "help," I spent the afternoon staff meeting proposing the exact opposite—that our Jackson, Michigan church compile a team of professionals to send to New York City.

This wasn't the first far-fetched idea I'd pitched in this setting, of course, as I had always viewed staff meetings as a good place to brainstorm the best way to save the world. But it was perhaps one of the first outlandish ideas that survived more than thirty seconds after leaving my mouth.

I'd like to say the idea was taken seriously because of my articulate delivery. But I think people are just a little more willing to entertain far-fetched ideas in times of crisis. After all, outlandish or not, few people on staff or around the nation could watch the footage coming out of New York and the Pentagon *without* wishing there was some way to be of some small help.

No one on staff even bothered with the usual polite dismissals. No one had the heart to say no. So I, of course, took that as a yes.

That day we did what nearly every church in the country did. We opened our sanctuary, midafternoon, for spontaneous prayer. On an average week, like almost any week that preceded September 11 in our lifetime, residents probably would've been more likely to respond to a fish and chips special at the local beach bar than to an opportunity for midweek prayer. But on this day the other events on our agendas seemed less important than when we had written them.

Next to the towers crumbling, "pick up the dry cleaning" became a trivial note.

Within minutes, a steady stream of people from across the county began flooding into the sanctuary. A tiny bit of sad perspective flooded in too, as my friends and I noted that we could not recall such widespread willingness to break from hurried life to pray at any other point in our lives. But unusual or not, by late afternoon, burdened silhouettes of Jackson residents filled the chairs—sitting, leaning forward head in hands, and even kneeling. I could not remember the last time I saw someone break away from social norms to kneel while praying either.

But that's what pain does. It can open things—church doors, minds, hearts, and even possibilities.

The sanctuary that enveloped the pray-ers was not the familiar layout of mainline churches with tall wooden crosses and baptisteries lined with fake floral arrangements. Instead, the dark burgundy walls stretched up to a black ceiling, uninterrupted by typical stained glass windows—or windows of any kind. The scrolling black stage that scaled the front wall was lit by dozens of white candles. Pillars, votives, and tea lights were grouped haphazardly about the stage, reflecting the disarray and general unpreparedness of the nation, and of those of us who scooped up old candles out of backroom closets for a makeshift prayer session.

Despite the unconventional backdrop, the blend of modern and ancient imagery seemed appropriate. In a technical age where war involved aircraft crashing into skyscrapers, it made sense to pray from such a modern setting marked by just a hint of flickering ancient church traditions.

While the community continued praying, I ventured into my office where my brilliant plan was to email and call every single New Yorker who I could find on the Internet. I wrote passionately supportive letters to complete strangers—executive directors and mid-level supervisors and secretaries and assistants who staffed human service agencies in and around New York City—searching for an opening, a crevice in which to grow.

2

MY OFFICE, WHICH BECAME THE MAKESHIFT HEADQUARTERS FOR A snowballing relief operation, also seemed like the right place to house such an idealistic campaign. Its bright orange walls, which refused to blend with the otherwise taupe and burgundy palette of the church's adult décor, reflected the sort of hopeful, buzzing energy most common to kindergarteners and other spastic souls who still believed in miracles.

My fiancé, Chuck, and I and a few straggling volunteers watched a miniature TV intently, as stories rolled in from Ground Zero and the Pentagon. Reports suggested relief workers would soon need a larger support system of reinforcements to sift through a disaster of this magnitude. But the newscasters' tone was optimistic. There was a steady sense that each new need would be met by people like us, waiting to be called from homes and churches and workplaces across the country. The footage of the towers collapsing had awakened our collective compassion like Bloody Sunday photos pressed onto the front pages of newspapers had moved the public to action decades earlier.

Jackson was no exception. The immediate and generous response of our small city, which—on a normal day—is six hundred and fifty miles from Ground Zero, made it seem like New York was our next-door neighbor. Thus, by the time all the follow-up emails and phone calls had been exchanged and we announced our clearance to help man the Salvation Army's relief stations in New York, Jackson was falling all over itself to support our new endeavor.

Before this point, recruiting volunteers or donations for service projects sometimes felt more like asking people to give up vital organs while they were still living and in need of them. After the towers fell, however, asking for help became akin to asking people for a simple cup of water. Residents arrived weighed down by armfuls of donations, as if the items they were bringing in poured out of their faucets at no charge.

Before we realized how pain was compelling our community, we compiled a basic list of requests, asking for inexpensive, easy-to-come-by items like thick socks and gloves for firefighters digging through the rubble. But I began to sense the community's heart had grown three sizes, like the Grinch who gained perspective on Christmas Day, when the first problem that arose was not a lack of socks, but the need for a bigger truck to transport the tsunami of socks that flooded into our makeshift warehouse within hours.

It was difficult to imagine how we had generated so many socks in a town I was not even sure sold this many socks in all our stores combined, until I talked to a lady from a nearby school that had been contacted by our volunteers. Children from the area community schools had rallied their parents to the biggest bout of sock-purchasing Jackson had ever seen. If you could've walked into our makeshift warehouse that afternoon, you might have guessed Jackson was the sock capital of the world.

Socks were not the only contribution either. Thoughtful people —the type of thoughtful I hadn't known existed—who I had never met before began hearing about our efforts through word of mouth and arriving in the middle of the day just to ask if I needed copies run or papers stapled. I have never in my life, before or since, seen people drive across town on a whim to staple paper for a stranger.

In just hours we had a several-member volunteer phone crew who provided information to relief team members and mediated needs between New York City and Jackson. Because of them we were able to pull together a trip so well thought out, complete with safety cards and ID badges and bundles of maps, that it seemed we had been planning it for years.

And the volunteers did a lot more than staple.

Psychology professors at the local university provided crisis training to our entire team free of charge on one day's notice. Electronics companies offered us walkie-talkies so our leaders could stay in contact. Doctors' offices shipped down pallets of saline solution to wash the dust and chemicals from the eyes of rescuers. A charter bus company offered us a free, fully-equipped vehicle with a driver and donated all of the gasoline. (You know you are experiencing a miracle straight out of Eden when gas is free.)

Even things that normally would've become obstacles were washed away by the community's outpouring of generosity. Before we left for New York, for instance, I learned that specialized masks with a particular kind of filtering system would be needed once we were on site, in case anyone in the group was stationed near asbestos dust or other dangerous chemicals that stirred from the rubble. When my initial calls turned up only a few of these masks in the local area, I sat stumped in my bright orange office, worrying that the volunteers I was taking would all suffocate to death when we got there. Meanwhile two construction workers who attended our church hunted down dozens of masks from across the state and then purchased and picked them up within twenty-four hours. They did all of this without being asked and without expecting a cent in return.

I felt like a follower of Jesus in that moment, who had the surplus of the kingdom at my fingertips—the feeling the Bible suggests the early church felt in Acts 2 when the needs of anyone who lacked were met by those who had excess. I felt like I was in my grandmother's garden and Eden had not deteriorated completely after all.

3

As we prepared to leave, the media continued to tell a sad story: Our nation had fallen into a tough spot. But when we arrived, it was instantly obvious that Jackson, Michigan was not the only town hoping to help grow something good from the difficult surroundings. Communities from all over the country had sent donations, so much so that—by the time we arrived at the Salvation Army—there was a miniature skyline of paper towel towers and water palette buildings lining both sides of the street.

A cheerful but exasperated Salvation Army worker met us by throwing up his hands into the air, as if this was the standard greeting that had replaced a normal hello and wave. "It's coming in from all over the country faster than we can sort it," he explained between hurried breaths that made it sound as if he had just finished running an obstacle course through the donation piles. Before he could say much more, however, he was pulled away to deal with a newly arrived truck of sack lunches packed by a nation of Girl Scouts, which were going to go bad within the day if not delivered.

I don't even remember anyone assigning our first task. The task, of course, seemed obvious. Something had to be done with the piles of random items accumulating in the streets before the current sorters were swept away in a landslide.

We didn't have experience sorting through donations of this magnitude. But, fortunately, in emergencies, you don't have time to realize what you don't know; you just move forward on the skills you do have. As a result, small-town Michigan housewives and nurses and high-school teachers became instant shipping workers, making split-second decisions about things they'd never done, like loading and wrapping pallets and correctly organizing the weight in trucks. We created makeshift assembly lines along the sidewalk to get goods on the semis, a system that served us well enough—despite at times blocking the sidewalk. Fortunately, the local New Yorkers didn't seem to mind the obstacles on their walkway. Several even stepped out of their busied stereotypes and into our chain of arms, passing along boxes without breaking stride as they passed by on their way to work.

Down at the actual Twin Towers site, blocks away from the Salvation Army, the sandstorm of need blew wildly. The typical buzz of New York's streets had been replaced by the steady crank of machinery and generators—a rumble that we adapted to surprisingly quickly, like the tick of a clock you didn't even hear in the background.

Nothing was as it was just a few days before.

Any other day, for example, this much chaos and effort would've signified some sort of city festival. Now, a street fair of blue and white tarped tents lined the sidewalks to serve as a makeshift town, ready to shelter the nearby relief workers with food and services. The ground that would've normally been kept clear by city sanitation workers, if not for an occasional stray leaf or peace of litter, was dusted with a thin coating of shredded paper and glass particles, as if a local Office Max had been incinerated and its contents dumped on the scene like unwelcome confetti. Even in the blackness of night, the usual darkness peppered only by lit windows of towering buildings was gone. The city was kept in a perpetually awake state by stadium lights erected as a substitute for the sun.

After a day or two of sorting at the Salvation Army, I was scheduled to the night shift at Ground Zero. The moment I got into a white unmarked van that would take me over to the site of the two fallen towers, my normal life routines were instantly replaced with the tasks of a character living in the wake of every disaster movie I had ever watched.

Waiting to cash out at the grocery store became standing in line for clearance checks, which seemed to be manned by a new agency every day—the Military Police, FEMA, or the NYPD. Zipping from place to place in my tiny Nissan Sentra became hitching rides—something my parents had told me never to do—on passing military vehicles in order to get to and from the tented Salvation Army canteen unit where I was stationed. And the props and balloons and music of our hometown children's ministry were replaced by a large upright cooler full of more freezing water than ice, which I dove into—up to my shoulders—to retrieve Red Bull and Gatorade that disappeared into the hands of firefighters and policemen as quickly as I fished it out.

Standing there in soaked rain gear, shivering, my voice jumbled through a weighty mask, I had some of the most compelling conversations of my life with people who became close friends out of necessity rather than through years of passing each other in the hallway each day. I quickly developed a particular fondness for the police detectives who maintained the makeshift morgue, which didn't get as much traffic as some places since the bodies recovered were few and far between. This unit became my immediate favorite after the first night, when a few of them arrived at my refilling station in a Jeep to give me a pair of shoulder-length gloves, a hardhat, and a lightweight filtering mask that I could more easily speak through. And they recruited me to bring them drinks in buckets, even passing on a Navy sweatshirt and a police-issued hardhat to allow me easier access.

My job was not to be the hero digging people out of rubble, but, much more simply, to help quench their thirst for water and human connection amidst the desert winds. After all, seeds need water to grow. And as often works when you set out to be the deliverer of help, I was able to find a crevice to crawl into where I could grow myself.

4

IN THE FIRST WEEK AFTER SEPTEMBER II, IT WAS MY DAD'S DREAM come true: It seemed like every human on the plant had become a New York Yankees fans. During the downtimes at Ground Zero, longtime Cubs and Braves fans could be found saying, "Wouldn't it be nice if—after all this—the Yankees won the World Series?" And then they would add, "Just this year though."

Unfortunately, the Arizona Diamondbacks later determined that New York's comfort would not come via Major League Baseball, as they defeated the Yankees in the best-of-seven series that November.

At the time, though, it seemed like everyone wanted New York to find some small good to tide it over until the city could flourish again. Emergency personnel, of course, worked through the night and through the day and through the next day, logging weeks worth of overtime they'd never be paid for. Department store chains sent their delivery trucks to transport literally tons of bottled water to the disaster site. Cruise ships arrived in the harbor to feed and house volunteers, cell phone companies handed out free phones to relief workers so they could keep in touch with their families, and therapists administered free counseling and even massages.

I could not believe that in this unlikely patch of ground, what was growing reminded me so much of Eden.

One of the things I loved most was that there was no rank or position. No one snatched me up, annoyed that a twenty-three-year-old church worker from the Midwest was pretending to lead an emergency team. Instead, every person—even save-the-world, fresh-out-of-college grads, and maybe *especially* them—was expected to shoulder responsibilities they had never rehearsed before. Hence I found myself coaching people on how to wrap pallets of water in some sort of industrial cellophane I had never seen before and writing supply requests on the back of napkins for Wal-Mart drivers who were listening intently as I listed off all of the drinks the emergency personnel craved most.

After a few days, even celebrities began showing up. People such as players for the New York Jets and the cast of *The Sopranos*. No one, of course—not even the Jets or nearby New Jersey mobsters—could put the towers back together, but they offered a much needed window of distraction from the sadness.

At one point, I told one of my regulars—a graying, middle-aged fireman old enough to be my father—that some movie stars had arrived and were giving autographs.

He looked at me for a long second as if I had just given him the most useless information of his life. Then he took off his hard hat, handed it to me, and said, "You came all the way from Michigan to stand out here in the cold every night—I'll take your autograph instead."

He became my favorite customer in that second.

Several days later, international help started arriving—firefighters with thick British accents and donations of food and blankets from Middle Eastern countries that the average American probably couldn't find on a map. "We tried to leave the moment we heard," one man told me in a heavy accent whose origin I could not have guessed. "But we waited in the airport for two days until your government cleared the airspace over New York for arrivals."

The other one nodded. "We left on the first flight they sent out."

This is how people grow, running into walls, but helping each other up to grow again.

5

I FIRST ENCOUNTERED THE PHRASE, "THERE ARE NO ATHEISTS IN THE foxholes," in my high school history class. At the time, I wasn't sure how accurate it was—whether atheists really found God in the trenches or whether that was just something Christians said to be clever. I know some pretty smart and stubborn atheists who might disagree with that generalization. But whether or not that is always true without exception, after spending a week on the site where thousands of lives had been lost, I understood why some time in the trenches might reignite some people's search for a god.

I don't know who among us had faith before we arrived, but it seemed as if nearly everyone found it or recovered it somewhere in the crevices of Ground Zero.

The relief workers on site were stretched to exhaustion as we forced our eyes awake at night—days after the last survivor had been found, but still days before all the searching would end. Regardless of your prior beliefs, when you find the end of your own energy supply, it is at least tempting to look for some source of renewal outside yourself.

This is why I often found myself praying furiously—as I had in childhood—for things like the safety of firefighters who refused to stop searching for fallen comrades even as rain poured down on the wreckage. I begged God not to let them slip to their own impalement.

In the evening, there were eerie stretches where I would slump onto a public park bench, take off my hardhat, and cradle it in my hands, longing for a few moments of the normalcy that now evaded us. As I stared at the towers, or rather at the mess of concrete and steel where the towers used to be, even the military planes that patrolled overhead reminded me not of safety, but of the two planes that had delivered this devastation just a couple days before. Even my prayers were sometimes interrupted by the unidyllic blasts of a bullhorn warning that parts of the tower might crumble further, in which case we were told simply to run in the opposite direction.

But we clung to any faint glimmer of faith and hope that arose—no matter how small—like a scraggly cat that emerged from the building's wreckage, which we hoped might suggest a few people inside might somehow be alive too. A wishful thought passed along the rumor mill was that they would uncover a pocket of air space somewhere in the lower levels, perhaps near the cafeteria, where groups of people would be found alive and well.

While the tower lay in pieces, shreds of people's lives lay exposed in Union Square as stunned family members frantically searched for news of their loved ones. Hastily photocopied posters bearing snap-shots of their relatives stared out from anything that tape could stick to. Storefront windows, glass doors, and even stationary vehicles became bulletin boards for the missing.

Over time these same family members lit thousands of candles, transforming the posted photos into a swelling shrine to the lost. Teddy bears and baseball caps and tiny crosses seemed to grow up from the ground, like roadside memorials that mark the scenes of traffic accidents, in a silent collective admission that the disaster had claimed its first victims.

A delirious Woodstock of guitar strummers, street preachers, and quiet worshipers sat cross-legged on blankets in open spaces near the shrines. People prayed loud, open prayers and messy, snotty-nosed weepy ones and quiet, lip-mouthing ones, voicing words they hoped would help birth new growth from life's hardest and most unlikely places.

Talk about God was as common as talk about the weather.

Questions like "Why did this happen?" and "How will we go on?" became the standard replacements for the usual "How are you?" and "Nice day we're having" greetings.

Chaplains had their own booths where relief workers could come for prayer, but they spent more time traveling among the makeshift tents, accepting invitations from various squads who didn't mind the presence of someone close to God in such a time. Another Christian agency printed pamphlets—full-color brochures with firemen and flags emblazoned across its pages—that offered comforting verses of care and support. The pamphlets, which most people, including myself, would have rejected had a passerby forced them into our hands September 10th, became instant bestsellers as of the 11th. They were scooped up by the dozens.

I'm convinced God was there somewhere too, browsing about the tents and the conversations, reuniting with people he had not talked to in ages and lapping up quality time with others before the moment passed and our to-do lists invited us back into oblivion, to routine tasks like picking up dry cleaning and washing our cars.

But for the moment, in the skeleton of life left in the tower rubble, everyone had the time to reflect about life. We had, as a generation, been detached from the comfort of our past in just one day. And now we were drifting, fallen seeds learning to grow in even life's hardest soil.

PART V

Dandelions, as members of the species *Taraxacum*, have the ability to reproduce asexually. Or to say it more plainly, each individual plant can reproduce by itself, without the aid of a mate.

But while their ability to reproduce autonomously makes dandelions well suited for survival, their self-sustained growth doesn't always work as planned. A dandelion with faulty genetic material may pass on its own flawed DNA to its descendants. With no source of healthy genes, the next generation is doomed and the growth that results is short-lived.

1

SOME PHYSICAL PAIN IS IMPOSSIBLE TO MISS. IT THROBS AND PULSES beneath your skin like a living creature that wants to rip free of your body.

But other pain is less forthcoming, producing only a dull, unimpressive sort of ache, like the kind that has taken up residency—perhaps bought its dream house—in my lower back. This is the type of pain you almost forget about, which is why even at twenty-five, I had never bothered to mention it.

One doctor, however, finally caught on.

"You have back pain, don't you?" she asked, as she eyed my spinal column.

I stared at her blankly.

There *was* a somewhat lackluster back pain so integrated into my movements that I barely thought about it most days. "A little."

There was a slight pause as her brow wrinkled. "Hmmm." She pressed her fingers along my spine. "Hmmm," she said again, in the exact way patients do not want doctors to *hmmm*.

"Has anyone ever told you that you have scoliosis?"

I shook my head no.

"Well then, *I'm* not going to be the first to tell you," she declared, bizarrely, as if her stealth *hmmming* and hypothetical questions didn't just give away her secret diagnosis.

Two years later, a second doctor—who was also *not* looking for spinal curvature—asked the same question, almost word for word.

"Anyone ever mentioned you have scoliosis? I don't see it on your charts."

Well, that's because Dr. Hypothetical didn't bother to write it on there. "One lady," I reported. "Sorta."

"Yeah, well, I'm surprised no one's ever had you look into it. I'm not going to write an official diagnosis, but you might want to look into that curve in your spine. It may not bother you now, but it will probably bother you in the future."

He was right. The back pain didn't bother me. What bothered me were doctors who seemed to be leaving me clues so I could one day solve the mystery of my own back pain.

* * *

AFTER MY SECOND ALMOST-DIAGNOSIS, I DECIDED TO GO TO THE chiropractor, out of curiosity—not just about my possible scoliosis, but about what exactly chiropractors do. Some people swear by chiropractors. They say that once you go, you'll never stop, as if chiropractors are the new meth. Other people, like my friend Jennie, tell me horror stories about errant chiropractors—not like the ones who would work with me, she was sure—who snapped patients' arteries. Accidentally, of course.

I decided to get to the bottom of the matter.

My first visit to the chiropractor's office was just a consultation, which in my doctor's mind meant X-rays and an evaluation of my condition. In my mind, it was primarily an excuse to get inside—the stealth move of a spy investigating what the sneaky art of chiropractic care was all about.

When I walked into the simple gray modular that housed the office, I got right to work on the case. First, I generally judge the worth of doctors and dentists and oil repair places by how many magazines they have in the waiting room. I especially like *Real Simple*. If someone has this, I'm in.

Then, I check to see if anyone in the practice graduated from medical school.

The next thing my investigation revealed was a cushy foam pad attached to one of the seats in the waiting room. I nestled into it, wondering if this alone might somehow cure my has-it-ever-been-mentioned scoliosis.

That's when I saw it: the deal closer. A bowl of red-foil-wrapped Hershey's Kisses—the kind made from dark chocolate with cherries inside. I promptly ate more than is socially appropriate to eat in a waiting room ... for evaluation purposes, of course. After all, good research must be thorough.

The presence of chocolate in the waiting room spoke well of the doctor's philosophy, I noted. I too believe the treatment for any illness, including back pain, should always involve an ample supply of chocolate.

Once I was escorted back to an exam room, I told the chiropractor that several nonchiropractic doctors have hinted, in a round-about way, that I may or may not have something resembling scoliosis.

He asks about my back pain.

"It's not a very impressive pain," I admit. Really, I wouldn't have come to see you if it weren't for all the rumors going around.

But yes, there is pain. The kind you get used to and accommodate. The kind you can pretty much ignore.

The doctor says this is not uncommon. "When you live with pain your whole life, or for long periods of time, you don't know what it is like to live without it. It just becomes normal."

The doctor then takes a few X-rays, which determine there is a lowercase "s" in my spine where there was supposed to be a lowercase "l." This typo on my backbone is the final clue, apparently. The rumors are true. I *do* have scoliosis.

The doctor then explains exactly what scoliosis is, or at least that is what I think he is saying. I am somewhat distracted by the remaining Hershey's Kisses in the lobby, which are calling out to me. Lovingly.

When I get home, then, I have to find out what the disease is all about, so I start Googling. I don't know who would suggest Google *isn't* a reliable source of medical information. I wouldn't even go to doctor's offices if it wasn't for the magazines and candy.

Just as scoliosis had evaded many a doctor's diagnosis, however, it also seemed to evade any conclusive explanation. What caused it? There were only theories. An accident? Genetics? Poor posture?

I started sitting up straighter just in case.

The most informative data I discovered was a brilliant YouTube video called "Celebrities Have Scoliosis Too," which I'm pretty sure was made by a seventh grader.

The film starts with a touching introduction encouraging those diagnosed with scoliosis to be optimistic. I thought this part may have been more calming had it not been accompanied by one of those emoticons that looks like a smiley face screaming in agony.

The video then moves on to assert that Sarah Michelle Gellar has scoliosis, as if Buffy the Vampire Slayer having scoliosis somehow validates the disease for everyone. Or perhaps it is insinuating that anyone who has scoliosis can also slay vampires.

The movie shows several pictures of Sarah Michelle leaning either to the left or right in an open-backed designer gown, and her spine appears—if you squint enough—to be just the tiniest bit curved. I imagine the seventh-grade YouTuber *hmmming* about Gellar's photo and then writing Gellar to ask, "Has anyone ever told you that you have scoliosis?"

Profoundly encouraged by my newfound likeness to Sarah Michelle Gellar, I decided to give the chiropractor, who claimed he could teach me new habits that reduce pain and prevent further damage, another whirl. This turned out to be a mostly beautiful experience.

* * *

I CALLED THE CHIROPRACTOR'S OFFICE A *MOSTLY* BEAUTIFUL EXPERIENCE because it wasn't *all* soothing adjustments. On my next visit, for example, before I could even get to the Hershey's Kisses, the chiropractor strapped me onto a machine that seemed—at first glance—to be straight out of a low-budget horror flick.

This was not designed to torture me, of course, but to pull and stretch my back into submission. Or at least this was what I told myself to keep from screaming.

As I lay on the machine, my lower half swaying back and forth like it was on a hips-only amusement park ride, I checked for Igor lurking in the shadows throwing levers.

I wondered if I did scream if the doctor would pacify me with chocolate. The urge to scream, however, slowly dissolved as, to my surprise, the torture felt much better than I expected.

It almost felt—dare I say it?—*good*.

Before I could relax, however, the doctor moved on to his next trick.

"Wiggle your feet," he instructed, trickily.

I moved them back and forth, side to side, in circles. Small circles, big circles, ovals, diamonds. It was really quite fun.

This chiropractic stuff isn't so bad.

Then SNAP! While I was having the time of my life wiggling, the doctor abruptly popped my neck into place.

I was instantly offended. *Maybe I like my neck crooked, thank you.*

Next, the chiropractor had me lie on my side in a sort of aerobic crunch. I was told to stretch one leg straight out and pull the other up toward me like the stretch I could never master in ninth-grade gym class. Then—get this—he began jumping on me!

Well, maybe it was less of a jump and more of a lean-and-press sort of motion.

As I lay in the WWF ring being thrashed—I mean "adjusted"—I contemplated making a cracking sound with my teeth, hoping that fear of my spine splitting might cut short the infernal hopping.

That was when I heard what was beginning to become a familiar sound.

"Hmmmmmm."

There was more jumping, then a few seconds later, I heard it again, longer this time.

"Hmmmmmmmmmmmmmmmmm."

"What?" I demanded.

"Oh nothing."

But I was not born yesterday. Doctors do not *hmmm* at oh nothings.

Whatever was wrong with my back, however, was obviously something the chiropractor had dealt with before. He began rolling a little machine down my spine that resembled the way a hand mixer would feel against your skin. I am sure my body was being prepared for Frankenstein's dinner.

Am I about to be eaten? Am I dying? My mind raced.

"Stretch out your right leg," the chiropractor said. "Now your left."

I eyed him suspiciously, silently letting him know that his B-movie horror gig was up.

"Now stretch both legs all the way out."

I was sure he was measuring me for my casket.

I am dying!

Finally I'd had enough. "Look, just how bad is my scoliosis?"

In response, the chiropractor put my X-ray up on the screen and explained quite a few things in medical terms that made no sense to me whatsoever. I tried to pay attention this time, ignoring the tempting cries of the poor, neglected Hershey's Kisses.

It was difficult to focus with chocolate sirens singing in the background.

What I needed was the CliffsNotes version.

"Out of all the people who have scoliosis," I asked, "how bad is my case? Like out of ten—with one being 'we lied to you and you don't have scoliosis' and ten being 'you'll be paralyzed within the day.'"

The chiropractor said he didn't want to worry me, which of course worries me. "It's between a six or a seven," he says.

I quickly calculated that this meant I was in the top 30 to 40 percent of worst cases he'd treated, which made me feel slightly better. At least if I had to endure all this *hmmming*, I got to be at the top of my class.

As I left, I realized my back felt better than it had in years. I ate three Hershey's Kisses to celebrate.

I'm cured!

But as it turned out, I was not cured. In fact, my general lack of awareness made me a total slacker in the chiropractic health department. I was given some stretches to do on a plastic exercise ball, which I rarely ever actually do, and some gel-foam inserts for my shoes, which I rarely ever wear. I didn't actually *want* the shoe inserts. I just wanted to stand on the foot scanner, which looks exactly like the regular computer scanner on which I upload photos of my dog. On the scanner I could see infrared pictures of my foot in neon green with red and purple waves, as if my foot was at the center of a tropical storm.

This alone made me forget all about the back pain.

This is the way it goes with most of my weaknesses in life. I remember them, consider doing something about them for a while, but then they drift out of my mind as if some sort of genetic flaw has swept away my intentions.

2

PHYSICAL DISORDERS ARE ONE THING, BUT I HAVE A LONG LIST OF spiritual and emotional flaws that radiate steady background pain into my life as well. These dysfunctions are with me every day, just waiting to be discovered and rediscovered after I've forgotten them for the three thousandth time.

Someone might ask me, "Has anyone ever told you that you're stubborn?"

"Might" ask me. Hypothetically. Not that anyone has ever asked me that.

Or they could also possibly — in another fictional conversation in a pretend world — ask, "Has anyone ever told you that you always think you're right?"

Questions like these, of course, are as rhetorical as the doctor's hmmming. They are not really asking if I have this condition. They already *know*.

But as with my scoliosis, a clear diagnosis of pride doesn't necessarily lead to a change in my daily habits. Perhaps if there were some sort of soul scanner that printed brightly colored maps of my arrogance, I'd be more interested.

I'm capable of stuffing my flaws down into the bottom of my psyche where they get lost like the ChapStick and pennies that roll around the bottom of my backpack.

Beneath the healthy self that I try to project, these faults and weaknesses crouch and wait. I hide them beneath my standard jokes and warm wishes. Most days, I can ignore their existence and proceed as if I am entirely well.

But as my chiropractor hints, there are long-term consequences when we ignore pain. If I continue to ignore my scoliosis, do I really imagine that when I'm forty, or sixty, it won't be worse? Similarly, if I make no effort to strengthen my personal weaknesses, do I really think they won't infringe on my personal peace and well-being?

So I *think* about changing sometimes, but mostly when it's convenient and comfortable and tailored to my desires. Thankfully, my chiropractor recommended such a treatment. They call it massage.

Massage? Yes, massage—the one treatment I've gritted my teeth through regularly.

I know. It sounds difficult. But I keep at it, somehow, week after week, no matter *how* relaxed it makes me. My perseverance inspires a lot of people. They may even do a documentary about me soon.

It helps that while chiropractors are nice people, masseuses are *beautiful* people.

Just typing the word *masseuse* makes me happy.

I sometimes accidentally call them masseusists, which I know is not a *real* word, but it seems right: what they do is as artistic, and just as symphonic, as a violinist or pianist. I could listen to their concertos on my spinal cord all day long.

My first masseuse was a black belt of pressure points. Her curly-Q cheekbone massages and hair tugging made me delirious, afraid to get behind the wheel to drive home. She was conversationally perfect, too—not rambling on about the weather or how many potato chips her three children ate for lunch.

I like my massages silent and peaceful, which is a rare state for me, I'm afraid.

My husband and brothers have been looking for the antidote to my talkativeness for a long time. Lo and behold, the long-sought mute button is in my spinal cord. A little oil and a little pressure and I am as shy and reclusive as you want me to be. In a coma, really. A beautiful, chiropractic coma.

My second masseuse—don't ask what happened to Black Belt

... that would completely *unrelax* me — is fantastic too. Maybe even better. What I like about her is that she seems especially disgusted with the tension I carry. She grunts and sighs, as if the muscles in my back are old friends who have let her down. I often feel as if I owe her an apology.

Perhaps if I'd worn my gel-foam shoe inserts more she wouldn't have to work so hard.

In any case, I lay there, being massaged, content with myself and the world, praying fervent prayers of gratitude. *Thank God for scoliosis.*

According to my masseusists, my body has responded protectively to my spinal curvature. The muscles on one side of my body lock up with protective inflammation to compensate for the curve on the other side.

The problem is that inflammation doesn't *correct* the problem. It only *protects* the problem. The spine continues to sit, curve and all, cushioned by a mixture of swelling and tightened muscles that are trying to make things better in a well-meaning but entirely mis-placed way — like a toddler who tries to soothe his mother's head-ache by screaming "Twinkle, Twinkle, Little Star" at the top of his lungs.

This, I am afraid, is also how I treat nonphysical pain that arises from my own selfishness or inadequacies.

I exasperate my husband, for example, when he tries to help me do ordinary things like filling out automobile insurance forms. He told me, for instance, that the church where I worked was about three miles from our home, so I nodded in acknowledgment and then secretly scribbled down ten miles. I'm a zillion percent sure. After all, it takes ten minutes to get there, which is how residents of our state often measure miles — a great calculation when you're counting miles between exits along the highway, but not so helpful when you're meandering along city streets.

My husband tries to tell me that ten miles is roughly triple the actual distance.

But I am rumored to be stunningly stubborn and always right.

It might even be more like eleven miles, I think. I cross out ten and write twelve just to be on the safe side.

Months later I have a revelation, which is usually how my "flexibility" happens. While jogging near work one afternoon, I had to measure the distance of my run so I'd know exactly how much to applaud myself.

From our house to the church where I worked it was approximately three miles.

Here's where the story gets good.

I tell Chuck over dinner that *I* have made a discovery. You know how when you're driving slowly and stopping at lots of intersections, going a mile takes quite a bit longer than it does on the freeway? I mean, it can even take ten minutes just to get three miles!

Sometimes I think that if I were my husband, I wouldn't want to be my husband.

But for his sake and mine, I'd better learn. Because weaknesses just get inflamed if you try to protect them. The tragedy being, of course, that something, deep down, is still crooked.

Unfortunately, I need more than a masseuse to work this stubbornness out of my soul. I need a Confessor.

3

As a child, spiritual insights generally came to me at church during planned times of learning.

I identified these insights because an adult, usually reading from denominational Sunday school material, subtly clued me in by saying things like, "This has been a spiritual insight." It was not unlike when *Sesame Street* unnaturally interrupted the program to tell you that today's letter is the letter *K*.

As an adult, however, my best insights often spring from unplanned, ordinary moments—driving, grocery shopping, or sitting in a soft, canvas-covered chair on our enclosed porch.

From the porch, life—or at least the slice of life I can observe—seems to be mostly in order.

From this position, for example, I barely notice the backyard, which has been meticulously landscaped by our relentless Jack Russell terrier, Wrigley. Its best feature is a two-inch deep ovular track, which Wrigley painstakingly carved around the yard's perimeter. He runs the track pathologically, as if he is part of an elite canine unit and the well-being of the neighborhood and perhaps all mankind depends on it. I expect the track to one day wear down into a trench for his warfare against neighborhood squirrels.

As you can imagine, our neighbors are beside themselves in jealousy.

From the porch, I barely notice the front yard either, which conveniently allows me to block out the looming to-do list that goes with it. My husband and I sometimes pretend to check things off this list. We pretend to rake the leaves or, more rarely, we pretend to weed the garden. Or, in a pathetic attempt to embrace middle-class norms, I sometimes pretend to plant flower bulbs. I do this in ridiculously small increments, hoping it will magically transform itself into a landscape from one of the home and garden magazines I pretend to read.

The view from our porch, blessedly, ignores our own blighted yard and instead looks out over a strip of open property that adjoins our land but does not technically belong to us. Because I feel no sense of ownership and no demand to maintain this property, I can wipe my mind clean and enjoy the untamed beauty of its nature — flowering trees I didn't plant and rustic greenery I don't have to trim. I think of it as God's small gift to me, a piece of Eden that calls me out of a life lived mostly indoors and inside my head.

* * *

IT IS HERE, ON THE PORCH, THAT I DECIDED TO CONVERT MOST recently.

I say "most recently" not to discredit my original conversion that happened more than twenty-five years ago, but to acknowledge something for myself: After decades of living as a converted person, I am badly in need of further converting.

There are parts of me that still need changing, parts of me that should be confessed. Unlike the Catholic kids in my high school, however, I did not grow up going to confession on a regular basis. But now, I decide, it would be helpful to get into the practice.

The one-room porch is not a perfect confessional, I assess, but it will suffice. After all, I — the rebel Protestant — do not need a second room or partition to house a priest to go between God and me.

God likes to hear how screwed up I am firsthand.

My confession is not technically, immediately confession-like. Instead it begins, *I've been thinking, God.*

I am pretty sure God rolls his eyes in response. Like "here we go again, little one."

A person shouldn't really claim to be connected to you if they stay the same year after year after year. Should they? I begin.

I mean, serving lepers with Mother Teresa changed people. Marching with Martin Luther King Jr. changed people. Heck, even passing out hymnals or visiting hospitals with my dad would change a person, God.

So how could anyone follow you for years without changing?

I pause to wonder if God is impressed by my philosophizing.

I mean, we wouldn't accept such lack of change in the physical world, would we God?

Like what if, for example, Drew Barrymore didn't change from year to year? I ask, as if it is clever to bring up Drew Barrymore in your prayers. *If the little blond girl from E.T. still appeared to be six years old when she appeared with the rest of Charlie's Angels in 2003, our minds would be derailed by the discrepancy.*

I think even God likes an occasional pop culture reference to keep things interesting.

We would know something was medically wrong with her. People don't go twenty-one years without changing.

But somehow, many of us—and I'm not necessarily saying me—have been willing to accept this same lack of change in the spiritual realm.

I am getting closer to the confession point. But first, I point out a few shortcomings of others.

For example, I tell God, *a man can go to church his whole life and still be a bitter tyrant who disrespects women. Or a woman can serve in the nursery for decades and still be a gossip who thinks nothing of ruining other people's reputations.*

I wink then, like, *You know who I mean, God. Those types.*

As you know, I am not a man, nor have I worked in the nursery, so it's clearly not me we're talking about.

Yet have you noticed, God, how many Christians have no difficulty categorizing this man and this woman as persons of faith? Like faith is just some sort of social label that is in no way linked to transformation?

Fortunately, God always has more time than I do, so he waits until I've spit out everything I have to say, until I've judged half the planet and turned the world upside down with my philosophies. Then he just smirks at me as I sit and stew in my own convicting thoughts, and raises an eyebrow.

Like, *Are you done yet, child?*

I finally say that I am. And then I sit there on the porch and silently attempt to measure my own faith by how much *I* have changed over the years.

And I start to feel sick.

My faith, I knew, often just sat there, unused in the container of my body, putrid like water no one had stirred in years, and an equally unappealing discovery.

I began to think of myself as a museum. A terrible, obsolete, and tiresome museum that was nothing more than a stiff, shellacked collection of Sunday school prizes and witnessing bracelets from the 1980s.

My confession was getting closer then. It was sitting at the back of my throat, like a sneeze I was trying unsuccessfully to suppress.

I finally broke down.

I hate.

I hate, I hate, I hate.

I repeat this because I need God to understand that I am serious. The hate I was talking about wasn't a tiny, "acceptable" portion of hate—as if my soul were somehow accidentally blemished by tiny, almost invisible hate burrs that latched onto my socks in the woods.

No. I hated *for real*, the kind of deep-down hate that is simultaneously creepy and satisfying.

Like, you know that adrenaline rush you get when you build a strong case against someone who has wronged you? How with a few sleights of hand and twists of the tongue, you can turn people into monsters? Or failures? And then you can hate them for it? Yeah, I can get a little too into that sometimes, God.

I start to feel a little guilty then, a little ashamed for indulging my flaws, so I backtrack just a bit.

It's not like I'm a hateful person or anything though, God. I mean, it's only a tiny list of people that I permit myself to hate — carefully arranging their mistakes into withered, lifeless bouquets that I display on the shelves of my imagination.

In fact, God, if it scores me any makeup points, I really do dread the greasy residue hate leaves in my soul — the sticky, unwashed film that cries out for a scalding shower. Sometimes I cannot stand to be in the same room as myself, God.

Then I look down at the floor for a long time and, noticing the herd of dust balls migrating across the tile, I begin to berate myself for not cleaning more.

This is when God seems to give his next piece of profound wisdom. *Shut up already.*

Shut up, shut up, shut up.

In a rare moment of wisdom, I do what I am told. And then God seems to direct my gaze outside. Like, *Look around you, crazy person. I made this world for your pleasure, not for your self-loathing.*

I sigh and remember Eden one more time.

4

I SPENT THE FIRST FEW DAYS AFTER MY CONFESSION SECOND-guessing whether it was really *that important* that I change, as if letting God transform me were an optional sun roof that I wasn't sure was worth the extra five hundred dollars.

Some of my hesitancy, I decided, stemmed from the magnitude of change I was contemplating. This wasn't just being nicer to my husband when he leaves eight pairs of shoes by the door or being polite to the coworker who sends me four million email forwards a day. This was comprehensive, deep-rooted, sweeping change that, frankly, seemed like a lot of work.

I found myself wondering if God made a smaller transformation package available for lazy people.

And so my thoughts—or were they prayers?—would ramble toward and away from God as I sat on the porch night after night, constructing and deconstructing cognitive defenses. I was developing what I hoped was an airtight case to explain why my current state of being was actually—on second thought—perfectly acceptable.

So what if I hate a few people? I'm a nice person, I thought in my perfectly lovely voice. *I have a lot of admirable qualities. As evidence, I will now recite my character strengths for my own listening enjoyment. First . . .*

However, in the court of my front porch, which is where I had invited God to preside, my excuses were coming apart.

No matter how good or nice or smart I was, I kept returning to my original confession.

I hate. And even if there was just a shred of hate in me, it was still more than sufficient cause to change.

Not to mention, hate was only Exhibit A.

There were other exhibits in my embarrassing collection of failures—exhibits A through Z, and then exhibits AA through ZZ, and *then* exhibits AAA through ZZZ—all of which could be carted into court like the letters to Santa in *Miracle on 34th Street*.

I knew from the mission statement of the church where I had worked, which was based on John 10:10, that God did not want me to spend my life drowning in the consequences of my own flaws. On the contrary, Jesus had said, *I come to give you life and to give it to the full.*

This too seemed to suggest I needed to change. Because although I was convinced my life was blessed, it was not always all the way *full*. And I didn't want to send God the wrong message—that I was content with this amount of full, with half-fullness or three-quarters fullness.

As if God were a waiter asking whether to top off my coffee.

No, no, God. No more for me.

If there was a better way, a more blessed, more full way of living, I decided I wanted it.

So I said a sinner's prayer of a different sort. *God, I want to change—but this time, I want to keep changing.*

I find my prayers often spill out in a list of "want tos"—telling God what I *plan to do,* at least in my best moments, when I am most sane, when I have some leftover energy and some spiritual wits about me. That way, I feel he can respond graciously in my worst moments—like the teacher of the smart kid who intends to be good, but actually ends up being quite obnoxious most of the time.

The prospect of praying for ongoing change, then, is sobering. And so for the next few minutes I don't say anything at all. I just sit and stare out the porch window as if I am locking eyes with a visible Creator who just happened to be walking my strip of Eden at that exact moment.

Then I add one more thought.

Even though I want to keep changing, I'm pretty sure I'm gonna need some help.

With this in mind, in addition to requesting God's assistance, I also decided to recruit my friends.

PART VI

As a child, I pronounced "dandelion" as two words — "dandy lion" — as if the fuzzy yellow flower were akin to the bright mane of a cartoon king of the jungle.

As it turns out, however, the dandelion was not dandy at all. But rather the French named the diminutive flower *dent de lion* because its long, lance-shaped leaves resembled ferocious lion's teeth.

The dandelion, of course, would be wise to face even its less flattering side. Because it is only in knowing itself that the dandelion would realize it is capable of rising above the bad around it.

1

IT TOOK ME AT LEAST TWENTY-EIGHT YEARS TO REALIZE THAT FAITH should involve ongoing change. And another year to get around to changing.

Given my apparently slow learning curve, I was not willing to wait another twenty-nine to find out *what* I should work on changing. I figured I'd better step up the pace a bit.

So I decided to take a poll. About myself.

My survey participants would be whichever family and friends could be pressured into participating.

I started with my two brothers, David and John. My younger brothers, who I count among the greatest gifts of my life, came with fully functioning "honesty chips" preinstalled. They can be counted on to point out exactly what I should work on changing—pointing out, for example, when I have committed a tragic offense such as applying too much blush or wearing a stupid hat. (For the record, *any hat* that is not a baseball hat is considered a stupid hat.)

David is three years younger than I am, and John is eight years younger, though at six-feet-plus, we all seem to be the same age (or they're even older, as I tell them). We used to compete in backyard sports, but now the only real competition is between them—as in who can block my shots the hardest or drag me the furthest while scoring a touchdown.

I decided to poll my brothers about my weaknesses when they were playing a game of Madden Football on the Xbox 360. While this might be considered bad timing by some, I calculated this to be my best shot. After all, they're guaranteed not to move until the fourth quarter ends.

Conventional etiquette calls for introductory small talk before jumping into philosophy and self-analysis, but my video-game football knowledge is severely limited. Besides, my brothers — who grew up within earshot of my every verbalized discovery — are never surprised when I launch into a lighthearted dissertation on the implications of spiritual change, a subject that I find naturally complements any video game, as well as every other task from eating oatmeal to standing in line at the grocery store.

They always indulge me.

And by indulge me I mean they nearly ignore me, contributing stoic "huhs" and "uh-uhs," while continuing to mash the buttons on their game controllers with impressive intensity.

"So, speaking of Hail Mary passes," I say, "what would you guys say is my biggest flaw?"

Their response is a brief interchange about how the video game automatically downloaded Brett Favre onto the Jets' roster, even though he had originally been assigned to the Packers.

After some consideration, I determine this is not a cleverly coded answer to my question, but rather a nonanswer.

I decide to pick them off one at a time.

I start with John, hoping the baby will crumble first.

I repeat the question. "No seriously, what do you think is my biggest flaw?"

There is a twenty-second delay before the question is even acknowledged, as if John is on the other side of a canyon, rather than five feet away on the ripped orange vinyl chair that we keep only because it happens to be upholstered in one of the Fighting Illini colors, which renders it invaluable.

"I dunno," John says finally, or at least this is what I translate his unintelligible mumbles and shoulder shrugging to mean.

"I don't believe you don't know," I protest.

John has lived with my husband and me the last three summers, as well as for his last year of college, which I calculate is enough time for him to have observed at least *one* of my flaws. "You can tell me. What is my biggest flaw?"

To which John repeats, more insistently this time, "I don't know."

I switch to David then, moving away from John to give him time to think of his answer, like one of my students. David is the classic middle child; I can count on him to pacify me.

"Okay, okay, how about you, David?"

David also lived with us part of the time he was in college and we, being much closer in age, spent a good chunk of childhood together as well. I estimate that after observing me for twenty-seven years, David should be able to come up with at least *two* flaws.

"What's my greatest flaw?" I ask again.

David responds, rather surprisingly, that *nothing* really jumps out at him.

I'm flattered. *David can barely even imagine me having a flaw.*

But then he adds, "I mean, it's not like I sit around thinking about *all* my sister's flaws."

I immediately make a mental note to refer back to his use of the word "all" when deciding how much money to spend on him at Christmas.

"I mean if I had to choose *one*," David says, as if trying to sort through my myriad flaws that instantly flood his mind, "I would choose that you always think you're right."

And then David adds fairly, as middle children must *always* be fair, that he hesitates to mention this since *everyone* in our family always thinks they are right.

I nod, perfectly able to accept this. After all, thinking you are right is only a flaw if you *aren't* right.

John then jumps in: "I was going to say that you think you've thought through things better than other people."

I contemplate whether this is really a *flaw* or whether I am just admirably thoughtful. But I pretend to be open-minded. "So what would you call that?" I ask. "Arrogance?"

John says it's not *necessarily* arrogance because maybe sometimes I *have* thought about things more than other people. The flaw, he says, is that I expect everyone else to arrive at my same conclusion.

My immediate reaction, which only underlines his point, is to wonder, quite sincerely: *Well, why wouldn't they?*

This is when I write down *arrogance* under *always think I'm right* in the notebook.

Later I show my brothers my developing list of known flaws. I think I've been pretty honest and tried to identify even the tiniest and most well-protected flaws that might usually be considered blind spots.

My brothers scan the list without arguing or asking clarifying questions about any of the flaws I've listed, as if they're thinking, "Controlling ... check. Talks too much ... check."

Occasionally, they throw out a suggestion. "Hey, you don't have anything on here about being stubborn"—they flip the list over—"it must be here somewhere."

Although I was too stubborn to add that flaw previously, now that they're looking at me expectantly, I grouchily add it.

Then I remind my two brothers that some people in our small town comment that the three of us are alike—which makes this list partly about them as well.

I am a paragon of maturity.

2

Next I poll my husband.

Unfortunately my husband and my brothers get along marvelously, which means they have spent countless hours jointly giving me the thumbs down or declaring every suggestion I make is the worst idea they've ever heard—all things that they think are absolutely hysterical. They also do this to David's wife, Melissa, and John's wife, Jill—both of whom, like me, are quite tolerant of their teasing and only occasionally spit vengefully into their food before serving it.

Their latest gimmick is to pretend they are asleep, video game controllers and pop cans in hand, every time I come into a room where they are. This joke has been going on for at least a year and has yet to get old, because no matter how many consecutive times they use it, fake sleeping is apparently never *not* funny.

So my husband takes a long serious look at my list and says, "Well, I'm glad to see you've decided to change a few things."

This is a nice, affirming response, which is the sort of thing I'd expect from someone like my husband, who was born more relational than most people become in a lifetime. Unfortunately, his affirmation only lasts about two seconds.

"I mean, honestly?" Chuck lets out an incredulous laugh, "I've thought you needed to change some of this stuff for a long time, but I *never* thought *you* would realize it."

I force a fake smile, silently vowing never to give my husband the middle cinnamon roll again for as long as we live.

But I can't be too hard on him. After all, my husband is endlessly useful to me: as my own personal OnStar navigation system; my in-house sports commentator who offers twenty-four-hour sports coverage with customized explanations about things I don't understand; and most important, as the comic and carefree balance to my relentless overthinking.

I need Chuck and his honesty in ways I don't even fully understand.

Plus, I have to admit, some days Chuck's lot in life is not an easy one. Sometimes, I imagine, it is a bit of a chore to be hopelessly intertwined with a manic, aspiring saint—a wiry woman who seems to have an ancient soul and a childlike demeanor crammed into a 110-pound body.

Plus there's the *alleged* arrogance and always thinking I'm right thing.

All things considered, Chuck definitely has the right to laugh at my fix-it list. As long as he keeps the laughing brief, and at a reasonable volume.

After all, Chuck is the master at finding the comedic value in my seriousness. When I started a nonprofit called Portal Ministries, for instance, which felt like a visionary move, my husband lovingly referred to it as PortaPotty Ministries, which of course had a way of downplaying the coolness of my self-imposed executive director status.

My brothers get in on the act too. At the release event for my first book, my brother John made sure I didn't overdo my self-congratulation. After discovering a C. S. Lewis book on a nearby shelf that was priced at three dollars *less* than my *Dear Church*, he cut to the front of the autograph line and slapped *Mere Christianity* down with humorous indignation. "Your book is three dollars *more* than a book by C. S. Lewis?!! Who do you think you are?!!"

My husband and my brothers are my personality insurance policy. They make certain that I never impress myself too much, which protects me from becoming a completely unbearable human.

But just to further ensure myself, I sought out a few more opinions.

I AM BLESSED TO HAVE A GROUP OF FRIENDS WHO UNDERSTAND AND apply social norms. They dodge potentially sensitive topics—perhaps politics or age or weight or tragically mis-dyed hair color—and never mention the flaws that I'm sure everyone unanimously attributes to me behind my back.

In fact, some of my friends act as though they would rather take a bullet than even so much as *hint* at what I should or shouldn't do. They are the reason why it sometimes takes me until 4:00 p.m., when I get home from work, to notice that I've had a shrub-sized piece of broccoli wedged between my teeth since lunch.

Fortunately, some friends can be pressed into service the same way family can. At the top of my "like family" group are Jennie and Bethany, who are not only metaphorical sisters to me, but genetic sisters to each other. They were also, in the days before husbands, my roommates.

Together Jennie and Bethany have taught me many of the things that I may have missed by not having sisters of my own, things like how Ruby Red Squirt is superior to all other soft drinks or how when choosing chip dip, you should always look for sour cream in the ingredients. The best chip dips have sour cream, and the sooner you realize this, the better your chip-eating experience will be.

Jennie, who is the shorter but older of the two, claims she measures in at five-foot-one-and-a-half inches tall (the half inch being a fact she notes precisely, just as six-year-olds remind you that they are six-and-a-*half*). But her small frame doesn't stop Jennie from adopting a supervisory role—acting maternally toward everything that breathes, including people two and three times her size. Thus Jennie is always nurturing her "children"—meaning every other human or animal on the planet—toward health and well-being.

Jennie, for example, is the only person I know who has ever bought penicillin for a single goldfish. This, she would maintain, was because Samson, who was worth approximately fourteen cents US currency, was experiencing a health emergency. Or at least Jennie thought Samson *might be* experiencing a health emergency as she noticed he was getting slightly pinker than usual around his gills.

And maybe she was right. After aforesaid application of penicillin, Samson did go on to live an abnormally full and long life for a goldfish.

I figure with Jennie taking care of me I should live to be about three hundred.

Over dinner with Jennie and Bethany, I express my irritation with myself over not changing much in the past few years.

Jennie nods in affirmation—ever the perfectionist, she also always feels like there is more she could do.

When I run through my list of flaws, Jennie listens to my spiel with such intense agreement that I can tell she is already making her own list of things to change in her head.

Then Jennie and I do what we always do: overanalyze.

We banter back and forth, discussing everything we know about change, how transformation works in America compared to other cultures, how society has evolved throughout history, how change induced social reforms across history, how there are endless types of change—social, spiritual, educational, emotional, and so on—one can make, and if we happen to know the Latin or French root words for *change* or a relevant quote from some philosopher, we throw those in too.

We carry on like this for hours.

When our dialogue finally stalls—and both of us lie motionless on the couch, short of breath and physically incapable of speaking anymore—Bethany speaks up from the loveseat where she's been lounging silently for hours.

"I don't think you should be too hard on yourself."

"About what?" In my comatose state, I can barely remember what we were talking about.

"Demanding so much change of yourself. You're human. You're always going to be in process," Bethany says, as if she is a guru who sits atop a mountain waiting for people like me to make the grueling trek to ask a question.

Her point strikes me as both profound and annoying; I've just exhausted half the afternoon searching every nook and cranny of my life experience for answers and then Bethany just swoops in and says something so balanced and wise in a single statement.

"Well, why didn't you say that earlier?" I protest.

"I was waiting for the two of you to take a breath!" she says to Jennie and me, which is like saying she was waiting for Halley's comet to come back to Earth: it happens, but not often.

I laugh and remind myself to add *overanalyzes* and *bad listener* to my list of flaws as well.

I prize Bethany for the way she speaks her thoughts with less analysis than Jennie or I, as if perhaps humans do not absolutely *have* to dissect every thought that wanders through their heads.

I have yet to determine whether this is an equally legitimate way of handling things, but I hope exhaustive future analysis will provide me with a satisfactory answer.

Once, on a trip to Boston, Bethany's honesty changed me in a fundamental way. In a trendy, overpriced dessert bar, Bethany called me out for being unable to express my emotions in a healthy way—emotional baggage from my recent job resignation kept me from fully enjoying the trip, a fact that bled onto their own enjoyment as well.

Worse yet, I barely realized I was acting any different.

Our twelve-hour trip home was virtually silent as I mentally rehearsed a long list of reasons why I was right and she was wrong.

But in the months that followed, I admitted to myself that I respected Bethany so much that I could—that I should—allow her to speak truth into my life.

And so, despite some resistance, I let the seeds of her comments take root in my soul and I began to learn, if only in small ways, how to be at least slightly more aware of the ways that my emotional life affected my family, friends, and coworkers.

I always knew that smart people listen to their friends; I'd just never bothered to do it.

4

MY MOST RECENT FRIENDSHIPS ARE WITH FELLOW TEACHERS. To students, the idea that teachers can be friends with each other seems impossible, as they cannot picture teachers having friends to begin with. If our students could see teachers being normal humans—letting loose at holiday parties or heckling an ump at a Tigers' game, they might fall over dead. Instead, students imagine that their teachers sit around and grade papers together, perhaps pausing for just long enough to look at each others' red-pen collections before turning in at our 8:00 p.m. bedtimes.

Nevertheless, during the single year I've been at my current job, I've formed some significant friendships. When you know that your coworker's boxer-terrier mix is named Tsavo, and that it is pronounced Sah-Vo but spelled with a silent *T*, you know you're on the right track.

Tsavo is owned by Mike who, besides teaching English and Social Studies directly across the hall from me, lives only one block from our house. This means we are *double neighbors*.

The defining factor about Mike's house is that everything in it—the cloth placemats, the letter opener, the salt and pepper shakers—has been carefully placed in position at the exact latitude and longitude that Mike prefers for it.

I wouldn't be a bit surprised to learn that he has a graph-paper map that records the exact coordinates of all his possessions. And if he doesn't, he probably should, seeing as I spend most of my time in his house trying to displace objects without him noticing—exchanging a picture frame on one side of the room for a vase on the other or scooting his stack of incoming mail a destabilizing six inches to the left of its original location.

Thankfully Mike has a sense of humor, which allows him to laugh through gritted teeth as he returns everything to its proper place.

One day over the phone I tell Mike about my list. He's the perfect kind of friend to tell since he's actually interested.

"Read it to me," says Mike in his teacher voice.

"The first one is ... pride," I tell him.

Mike detours through a lot of *ahhhs* and *hmmms* before arriving at a response, which is, I think, cautious and slightly camouflaged agreement.

"What's the next one?"

"Overthinking things."

"I don't see anything wrong with that," Mike says, almost immediately. He is also a chronic overthinker.

"Yeah, me neither, but apparently there are other people who think it's a problem," I say with a laugh.

We continue like this. Each time I list a new weakness, Mike evaluates whether he finds it to be legitimate. It is as if he is scoring my identified flaws the same way he grades his students' essays.

Improve your topic sentence. Use specific examples, he writes in verbal red ink.

Mike always asks for the next flaw, partially because he's curious about my own development and partially, I suspect, because he's also grading himself. *Hmmm, I think I'm at least 10 percent better than Sarah in the listening department.*

This is another thing I respect about Mike: he wants to grow too. Recently, just two years after converting from a lifetime of atheism, Mike went on an outreach trip to Cameroon, where he dressed up as a human flashlight named Flashy to perform skits for the local children.

It is clear that Mike is light-years ahead of me in the humility department.

Mike, of course, is not the only coworker who blows me away in the humility department or who inspires me to change by his example, which brings me to Erik, one of the final friends to weigh in on my list.

Raised by a Harvard-educated lawyer, Erik is a liberal, political independent, and a diehard heavy metal fan who has Iron Maiden covers tattooed on his arms. Hence, there is some obvious contrast to my knee-sock-laden childhood nestled in the palm of the conservative Christian movement, singing along to children's worship tunes—the kind with hand motions.

Fifteen minutes into my first discussion with Erik at a coworker's holiday party, though, I'd already forgotten that any differences existed.

Discussion, in this case, is a term used loosely, as most of my exchanges with Erik lean more heavily toward sarcastic banter than polite dialogue. But that's not to downplay the quality of communication involved. If anything, our playful humor and wit probably escalated the pace and depth of our friendship. And, as a result, we've landed in plenty of brother-sister–like fights. We've also arrived at a level of ease that makes it okay when he comes over to play video games with my husband and walks right into piles of unwashed laundry and the empty pudding cups toppled over beside our bed. (These, I am compelled to mention, are on *Chuck's* side of the bed.)

One of Erik's decidedly best features is his wife, Jill, who is one part model and two parts rocker chick. Her eyes are drawn, like an eagle's, to anything purple or sparkly, and she has that enviable sense of self-assurance and coolness that lets her rock clearance items like three-dollar windbreakers and silver medallion earrings from a Meijer's clearance rack.

I also love that Jill is the opposite of controlling, letting her girls experiment with different hair colors—blue and green and pink—for fun and because, beyond fun, she believes in a broad definition of beautiful that lets people be themselves.

Speaking of her girls, I should add that I am also in love with Erik and Jill's daughters who are my fiercest competitors in summer games of I Spy. I love how crafty Mira changes her chosen objects fifty-three times to avoid losing and how mature-beyond-her-years Providence compliments other children on their excellent, but mistaken, guesses.

When you put Chuck and me in a room with Erik and Jill's family, our laid-back laughter makes me feel like we're a too-good-to-be-real sitcom cast.

I slipped my list across the table to Erik when we, along with Mike and our coworker and friend Andrea, were sitting in a coffee shop, ignoring a writing workshop we were supposed to be attending. Here is what he saw:

> Hate, grudges, monster creating
> Pride, criticalness, treating others as inferior or celebrating their failures
> Poor listener
> Selfishness
> Unhealthy boundaries
> Barriers with certain personality types
> Appreciating those I love
> Managing external emotions rather than solving problems
> Saying things with the motive of impressing others
> Not always taking responsibility for my actions
> Always thinking I'm right
> Overthinking things
> Buried faith
> Overthinking things (I wrote this twice, thus proving I can even overthink overthinking)
> Excessive accumulation of possessions

Erik responds like a doctor who isn't sure he believes all the reported symptoms. He makes me define each flaw.

"Why do you say you are arrogant?" he asks protectively—a question that a year later, he no longer asks for some inexplicable reason.

"Well, for starters, I think I'm better than you," I joke.

"Nope. Not buying it," Erik says bluntly. "Can you give me an example of that?"

Fortunately, I can rattle off about four hundred nonnegotiable examples of my arrogance in action. But still, in the end, Erik insists that my list of weaknesses doesn't describe me at all. "Seriously. These sound like a different person," he says. Secretly, I love him for saying that.

I immediately warn Erik: "Nope—it's me. You'll see."

Erik closes my journal harder than necessary, as if he now considers it an enemy. "You're fine the way you are. What's a flaw, anyways? Isn't everyone's definition of *flaw* different?"

But I've come too far with this change thing to take the attractive escape route he's offering me. Sure, I could second-guess my list. I could question if I'm really all that messed up. I could doubt that my flaws are *really* as serious or as numerous as I think. Even my closest friends would let me off of this hook most of the time.

There's one problem, though: I am starting to *want* to change. I am beginning to believe I can live a more ideal life. That I can experience even more peace and well-being. I think I can almost see Eden on the horizon.

PART VII

In America we have uncreative uses for the dandelion. We mow them down mostly, or at best, we help our children string them into necklaces.

But some people get more out of the dandelion. For instance, did you know its roots can be used to make a sort of coffee that is said to be good for the liver? Or that they can be made into a bitter tonic that can be used as a laxative?

Even the dandelion seems to innately understand that purging one's unhealthiness is necessary every once in a while.

1

ONCE I FINISHED MY LIST, I DETERMINED TO BEGIN WORKING ON MY newly identified weaknesses. After all, I am no longer content with blowing aimlessly about. I need to purify myself, to rid my life of routine barriers to transformation.

I attack my flaws the same way I approach grocery shopping, organizing my list by sections. I use logic to plan my sequential path through the store — noting that green tea is by the produce section and that Doritos are by frozen foods and it's easiest to pick up pita bread on the way in since it's perched on the rack right by the automatic doors.

In a similar manner I decide that the "desire to impress others" is in a category near "pride," and that "selfishness" and "poor listener" are probably in the same department as well.

After a quick assessment, I pick what I hope will be the easiest place to start: "accumulating excessive possessions."

It's not that I expect this change to be *easy* because I am so divinely unattached to my belongings, but rather that I guess it might be easi*er* because I am more willing to part with a few extra bottles of nail polish than with my beloved pride.

I mean, the tangerine ice base coat has only sat in my closet for three months. But my superiority complex? I've been treasuring that my whole life.

To eliminate pride would be like killing a familiar old friend, so I push pride down to the bottom of the agenda.

There you go, pride — you'll be safe here.

I immediately focus on my seemingly straightforward goal. If I cut down the number of things I own, I will reduce the amount of time I spend trying to maintain them.

I swear, for example, that when I add new necklaces to my box, I lay them in carefully, as if they are goldfish who have been hooked from Claire's clearance rack and must now adjust to new water. I try not to let them touch. But without fail, when I come back, my necklaces are intertwined as if some Boy Scout snuck into my closet overnight to practice his knot tying.

Just thinking about never having to unwind these chains again gives me the vision to move ahead with my task.

I start by emptying all my possessions into piles on the bedroom floor. My original intention, of course, is to sort through the piles right away. But even getting all the items in one place proves exhausting. So instead, until I have time to get to them, I leave the piles lying near the door where I have to walk by them every time I enter or exit our bedroom.

It isn't long before I get tired of gazing at the messy little mountain range of my belongings. They are neither scenic nor practical, and they are difficult to cross. Going from the bedroom to the kitchen, I have to step over a gauntlet of old school supplies and makeup cases and plastic combs.

Sorting becomes like an audition. I allow each item to make a little speech as I consider how worthy it is. If an item makes the cut, it gets to move into a newly arranged, well-organized box or onto a clean shelf. But if the item is obnoxious or keeps saying, "Like, um, you know?" then I give it the boot.

Unfortunately I discover that I'm far too compassionate. No sooner do I kick some things out than I invite them back in. I look at them tenderly—*How could I stay mad at you?*

I can't help that I have a heart.

After all, it's not like the pair of sporty sandals *asked* to be bought. I bought them of my own free will—or at least of my *mostly* free will, since bright orange clearance banners bedecked with percentage signs have a special way of hypnotizing me. In any case, I am the one to blame. Why should the sandals be relegated to a secondhand store where they might be tried on by dozens of smelly feet?

Simplifying my possessions already seems less than simple. I sort through a pile of candles—an obscenely large pile, an "is she on the neighborhood emergency response team that distributes candles during blackouts?"—sized pile.

I consider applying for this position so I can justify keeping them.

The thing is, I *love* candles. I love the bright bold colors, the vanilla and almond scents, and the tiny pool of molten wax that is slowly gathered up into the light of the flaming wicks.

In my candle collection I notice a huge subcategory of orange candles. Since orange is my favorite color, any orange candle I find on sale seems like an investment that can't go wrong. I mean, really, who can *ever* have enough orange candles?

Oddly, though, I love orange candles so much that I save them for the most special of special occasions. What this means, practically, is that my best orange candles live in a plastic Tupperware container tucked beneath my bed.

As you can imagine, they bring joy to millions there.

Why do I own so many things that I never intend to use?

Why do I own a set of brown candles that look exactly like tree stumps? Why *anyone* would buy these is beyond me, but somehow—no doubt orange clearance tags were involved—I bought a set at an outlet mall. I mean, with the economy the way it is, that might have been my *last chance* to acquire such treasures at pennies on the dollar.

I decide, in the end, to donate them, trusting that some tree hugger will consider them a find. I hope this is a better alternative than chucking them in the garbage, which seems wasteful.

After all, there are people in developing countries who don't have the luxury of owning tree-bark candles.

Other items are hard to part with because of their place in my memory. My high school basketball team warm-ups *might* make sense to keep—you know, in case I join a community basketball team that just happens to be called the Summerfield Bulldogs—but why keep the reversible mesh tank tops we wore in practice? Shirts designed purely to absorb sweat are better left, along with the odor, in previous decades.

The importance of items like this to my memory is exaggerated, anyway. Even if I never saw another practice jersey as long as I lived, I would never forget all the "suicide" drills I ran all those years ago.

I throw the mesh jerseys into a donation box with some satisfaction. I am getting stronger by the minute. I resolve to be ruthless and not to keep anything stupid. This progress must continue.

Right after this resolution I uncover a squishy, plastic microphone that squeaks. This is emphatically *not* part of the stupid category, since my dog Wrigley's lip-synching just wouldn't be the same without it. After that comes a half-destroyed tennis ball, a mangled rope, and a supposedly lifelike squirrel developed to train hunting dogs, which Wrigley lugs around happily as if it is his mascot.

I suddenly realize that my dog has more toys than most children in the third world, which makes me feel like I am one of those clueless people standing at the foot of the cross. I say a quick prayer for Wrig's thirty-four toys. *Father, forgive me, I have no idea what I am doing.*

As I discover possessions I never meant to keep, I also find flaws that I've allowed to creep into my soul.

I never meant, for instance, to buy the idea that my identity is tied to my possessions. But while I was cleaning, I found it under my bed and on my shelves.

And I had thought I'd long-since pitched certain fears—like the fear that if I throw away certain cosmetic products, I won't be quite as beautiful—but it turned out some of them were still hidden away in the couch cushions of my life as well.

Weeding through *things* starts to feel like a purge, a spring cleaning for my soul.

After a while, I'm *almost* enjoying it. Soon I'm grabbing up items and shooting them at the garbage like I'm in a three-point contest. Bent bobby pins — swish! Broken eye shadow — swish! Pen with a fuzzy purple-haired troll on top — swish!

I also find some practical treasures. For example, I was absolutely *convinced* I needed to purchase more tupperware cups a while back, but it just so happens there are two-and-a-half sets rolling around under the bed! In another moment of triumph, I discover we have enough white and black socks to go a month without washing! And why is the unopened box of aloe-and-vitamin E-fortified Kleenex hiding under the yellow chair when I've been scraping my nose raw with generics all week?

I'm getting tired, but I reward myself with a pack of Rainblo gum that I found in my bedside table. I have no way to authenticate how old it is. But, after cautiously testing the purple one, I decide that it has not yet reached the danger zone.

I discover the orthopedic inserts that my chiropractor gave me. I was supposed to cut them to the shape of my feet and put them in my shoes, a task that I intended to accomplish right after I found my missing set of plastic cups.

I resolve that I will no longer own things that I do not use, and so I plant my feet firmly on the foam inserts and chop out a custom mold of my left foot which, I notice, looks like Illinois.

Soon I unearth yet another dog toy inside yet another plastic cup. I think of the children in Africa again, or even the children in some parts of the U.S.

God, don't strike me dead.

I eat the red Rainblo to comfort myself.

I begin to toss paperwork next, starting with the user manual for my phone. My little brother John is a living phone manual, and he's less convenient to dispose of.

I throw out a file of old credit card information, kept as if Uncle Sam might arrive at any moment and demand to know the APR of the Target card I cancelled in 1999.

I shred all these reminders that I lug my commercialism around like a ball and chain. I am annoyed at myself, annoyed at credit in general, and angry at what capitalism has done to our world. As each statement devolves into black-and-white confetti, I feel a little bit freer.

I eat another purple Rainblo to celebrate.

My piles of cast-off junk make my room resemble a landfill. If I grieve the loss of any of this, I tell myself, I am a moron.

I find an old phone cord, and we haven't owned a landline in years.

I find an inspirational bookmark that never inspired me. I throw it away without even a tinge of remorse, declaring that never again will I own anything uninspiring.

I toss coupons that expired in 2006.

I do not, however, throw out any chocolate. No matter how old chocolate is, I must keep it in reserve, in case my Rainblo runs out.

I plow through a pile of things I meant to scrapbook—pictures and concert stubs and airline vouchers for European destinations. I worry I kept these not to remember the trips—which I recall perfectly well—but to prove to myself how good and exciting my life is. From now on, anyone who wants to experience my thrilling past is going to have to free some time up to listen to my stories.

I hesitate at a collection of letters from previous bosses and scores from standardized tests for educators. These are portfolio pieces, evidence to marshal in case I need to prove my own worth. I determine that from now on people are just going to have to take my word for it.

I'm down to my last green Rainblo, which I chew slowly as I dump materials from mind-numbingly boring conferences, a pack of thank-you cards that are too ugly to send, and old school newsletters that never adequately documented what a privilege it is for students to learn in my classroom.

I toss old Christmas and birthday cards. I only keep a card if the person who gave it to me wrote something meaningful in it, or if the person who gave it to me is dead.

(If you're a friend reading this, I just threw down a gauntlet: If you want me to keep your card, write something meaningful, or die—otherwise your card is headed for the dump.)

Lastly, I hold in my hands a copy of my first book that is translated into Korean.

My publisher graciously sent me three copies of the Korean version, one of which I gave to Jennie and Bethany who stayed in Korea for a time and one of which I gave to my dad because he is so devoted to my publicity that he is probably even now marketing me in Asia. Now all of us have the same problem: we each have a Korean book and we don't speak Korean. I move it to the shelf in the basement, which serves as a book critical care unit, where literature goes to die.

My piles are sorted.

I feel a deep sense of satisfaction.

In this moment, on this day, I am free.

I determine to bask in this freedom for the rest of my life.

I will set new rules for acquiring more possessions.

I will retrain my thoughts and emotions not to crave unnecessary items.

I will hold with open hands the few possessions that I do keep.

At this rate, my slice of Eden is guaranteed to be beautiful *and* clutter-free.

Which is why I'm shocked, just six months later, when I notice refilled drawers and recluttered shelves and a bed propped up by unused possessions. I have no idea how these items found refuge in my house once again. I wonder if at night when I sleep my evil, yellow-sided house sends out some sort of homing beacon that calls its displaced furnishings and accessories back home.

And it is not just my resolve that I have lost. I have also lost some of the truths I discovered along the way. As it turns out, I, like the dandelion, cannot even seem to grow healthily on my own.

And so once again, I have changed, but I have still not changed enough.

2

I HAVE NOTES FROM EVERY CHANGE ON MY LIST, BUT YOU DON'T NEED to hear them all. The overall summary is that some changes went well, but others didn't, and almost all are still in process. Like the dandelion, I reproduced my own flaws a number of times along the way. And more purging is always necessary.

In the interest of time, I'm going to skip to the last flaw on my list. I know you're not supposed to have favorites, but I have to admit I had some special affection for this particular fault.

Alas, my darling pride, your time has come.

I knew letting go of my arrogance would require significant concentration, so I postponed confronting it until my next block of free time: spring break. My brilliant plan was to keep a journal in which I would record each instance of prideful thought or action while vacationing with my husband in Florida.

Little did I know they don't sell four-thousand—page journals.

I opened my new journal, enjoying the clean smell of possibility in its pages. I uncapped my pen, anticipating the words of wisdom and change that would flow from its tip. I took a cleansing breath and then, on the first line of the first page, I wrote—in flourishing cursive—"I am too prideful." Then—I swear this is true—I drew a smiley face next to it.

Sometimes I cherish my own weaknesses a little too much.

And so my week of the observation of my pride began.

We are at the beach, purposefully relaxing far away from the herds of tourists. We claim our spot in style, stretching out our blankets and strategically weighing down the corners with sandals. I ease out luxuriously onto our blanket, putting my ever-present iced tea exactly one arm's length away from me but far enough from the sand that it won't pick up any grit. I thoughtfully place my clothes over the suntan lotion so it doesn't overheat in the Florida sun. Everything is perfect.

For about two minutes.

A group of teenagers—or maybe they were college kids—playing football set up their field *right* by us. Like Chuck and I are the goal posts. I am instantly infuriated. There are *mammoth* stretches of untouched beach directly to our left, yet here they are. Can't they see me enjoying myself on my sand-free blanket? Don't they know I'm on vacation? Don't they know this beach is here for *me*? *Ignorant locals*, I mumble, *whose parents raised them with no manners.*

Later in the day, I cross paths with another inferior person, a boy at our hotel pool who uses his weight as a weapon—mercilessly trapping his toddler cousins with his belly and beating them with a foam noodle. His voice is a nasal whine, as if he's a sitcom character.

I fantasize about leaping into the pool and ripping the noodle from his piggy hands and meting out some vigilante justice, all the while accompanied by the appreciative cheers of my fellow sunbathers.

At dinner, the woman in the booth next to us keeps snapping at her daughter, Erika, who can do no right. Take the towel off your head, Erika! Stop playing with your cheese sticks, Erika! I picture Erika perched in a counselor's office, years from now, disheveled hair across her face, with a nervous twitch that begs for a cigarette, unable to meet the counselor's eyes.

Meanwhile, the woman orders her food, "I'll have the fish and chips and—Erika, God help me, I am going to beat you! Do you see how close the bathroom is, Erika?—do you have any chocolate milk?"

As I watch, I actually consider warning Erika's mother about the damage she is doing. You know, since I'm a parenting expert and the mother of as-yet-unborn children who are always perfectly well-behaved in my fantasy.

As I am writing all of this in my notebook the next day, Chuck doesn't seem to grasp how important preserving Erika's story is to my project. While I'm trying to concentrate, he keeps rotating his lawn chair to face the sun, a highly insensitive act that recasts the shade on my page distractingly. How am I supposed to work in such conditions?

At first, I try patience and humor.

Internally, I begin to call my husband the Human Sundial.

Chuck scrapes the metal lawn chair legs against the concrete deck a twelfth consecutive time, as if he is doing giant addition problems on a chalk board. According to his current position, and the shadows his chair cast on my paper, it is 3:00 p.m.

I try to keep myself amused. "Your new name," I tell Chuck, "is the Human Sundial."

I can immediately tell this was a mistake when his new nickname prompts him to make ticking sounds that are even more annoying than his former scraping sounds.

Chuck is enjoying himself, but I can't help it. I tell him smugly that *sundials* don't tick.

This is a normal interchange between us.

When Chuck and I vacation, we pack with the understanding that we won't be roughing it in the wilderness, but we'll be within close range of a Rite-Aid or Walgreens. However, even with modern convenience at our fingertips, there are still limits, right? For example, *twelve* iced teas seems like a bit much—a fact I enlighten Chuck about when he returns from the store, groceries in hand.

Chuck replies, underlining my rudeness, "You're welcome."

Did I mention he purchased the iced tea for me?

I do not let this curb my rudeness. Twelve iced teas? That's an average of four iced teas a day, I tell him.

"But it's 82 degrees."

I feel bad for a few seconds. He's thinking of me, his little wife, writing in the hot sun. He wants me to have all the iced teas I might possibly need.

I am a total witch.

I manage to smile politely and thank him, all the while secretly thinking that this is the last time I will ever send a ticking sundial to do my shopping. (Never mind that only a few hours later I'm starting my third iced tea.)

3

It's March 31, and Chuck went back to Rite-Aid for playing cards, which marginally annoys me. We buy them anytime we're without a deck, and hence we've collected several dozen sets at home in our closet, which we then forget to take on the next vacation. Maybe I'll wallpaper my house in playing cards the way my co-worker Andrea wallpapered her entryway with dictionary pages.

However, it does *not* bother me that I just bought the 3,047th ChapStick of my life—Lipsmackers Kiwi Strawberry—even though I probably have three tubes lost in the pockets of the suitcase that is five feet from me. ChapStick is entirely more practical than playing cards—and my purchasing choice is entirely superior.

Yet Chuck has the nerve to tell me I'm a hypocrite.

Almost instantly I admit he is right. I am a hypocrite. But I am a far better hypocrite than most people, I clarify.

I change the subject by telling Chuck that I have surveyed everyone else who is on our vacation, and they all want the Human Sundial to stop ticking.

It isn't hard to find something else that reveals my pride and self-centeredness. The hotel's Wi-Fi signal is weak. How am I supposed to email—er, work on my writing—without the Internet?

I blame the hotel and seriously consider asking them to refund part of our hotel room cost. I also blame Chuck, even though I manage not to say this out loud. Shouldn't he have asked exactly how strong the signal was in the various rooms and then booked ours accordingly? Sometimes I wonder how Chuck can live with himself.

It isn't until later that day that my pride starts to crack, when I see a small boy on the beach. He is tan and his tousled, coal-black hair shines in the sunlight. He is wearing only a diaper and toddling in the literal sense of the word, watching his feet with each careful step, as if he cannot understand why each foot depressed in the sand triggers a slight crunching sound beneath him.

For most of an hour he stands in the same square foot of beach, picking up handfuls of sand and letting the grains run through his tiny fingers.

I can't help but smile, which temporarily sidelines my prideful internal diatribe.

I notice, then, in the stillness of smiling, that the little boy did not judge himself, nor did he worry about whether he was being judged by anyone else who watched. In fact, whenever the little boy saw me, he would smile not in embarrassment, but in victory as if he had discovered something I might want to try.

The little boy was not my only invitation to embrace life rather than judge it. Later, I pass three more slightly older children burrowing depressions in the sand as tiny grains found hundreds of new passageways into their swimwear. They look up at us without embarrassment as Chuck and I pass by, not knowing or caring that uptight adults might judge their behavior inferior.

They are transcending judgment through pure naïveté.

That night my pride reasserts its primacy when my husband pulls out the wrong way on a one-way street after dinner. Chuck realizes we're headed the wrong way just before he turns, but in a split-second decision, he thinks he can make a quick U-turn back into the parking lot before oncoming traffic reaches us.

He's wrong, and as headlights bear down and oncoming cars swerve to miss us, I unleash a furious stream of superior words. He's already apologizing repeatedly, but he's hard to hear over the resounding gong of my righteousness.

Back at the hotel, I point out that hotel management could've picked better shampoo to stock the showers—apparently someone has swindled them into buying thousands of tiny bottles filled with colored water.

I head out to the pool to enjoy the warm evening, and it's as if I've descended into a three-ring circus of inferiority. I'm simply trying to enjoy the sun, and the local jokers are yelling out every disgusting detail concerning their variously injured toes.

Just when I feel perfectly happy with being perfectly alone in my rightness, I remember my journal. I suppose this might count as a tiny example of pride — feeling infinitely superior to an entire hotel full of people I don't know.

I write my latest prideful thoughts down and experience a small surge of pride for being so self-aware and willing to change.

So I write that thought down too.

And I wonder if this will ever end.

That's when I hear Erik's wry voice in my head. He tells me that I'm thinking things practically anyone would think. He says that we can't help but process our environment.

He says I shouldn't be so hard on myself.

I believe this is partially true, and so I let the fictional Erik keep talking while I nod sincerely.

But this Erik is in my head, so it's easier to get in the last word with him than it is with the real Erik. My thoughts, I tell him, are also a product of my own choices and habits. I've conditioned myself to think a certain way — and that means I can be reconditioned.

The fictional Erik rolls his eyes and mutters something about fairy dust.

I return my attention to the pool. Now the shouted conversation is about dirty socks. Before I can even roll my eyes, I put on my headphones to drown out my own judgmental stream of consciousness. By now I'm so tired from having to acknowledge my pride that I can't stomach even one more arrogant thought. I stop the thoughts just so I don't have to write them down.

This is a tiny bit of success, but I take it as evidence that I *can* change myself. I'm moving toward right again.

Bursting with pride, I celebrate by cracking open my thirteenth iced tea.

SOME DAYS I *DID* CHANGE. BUT OTHER DAYS, DESPITE THE GROWTH, I couldn't help noticing that I never seemed to kill off all the weeds in and around me.

I became aware of some of these lingering weeds while teaching at daVinci, a community-based charter school that housed 120 or so high schoolers on the campus of our local community college.

The school, housed in a somewhat utilitarian building, boasted an extravagant philosophy. Its visionary language, sprinkled throughout speeches delivered to students in daily "town meetings," expressed a desire to be a school that valued "human dignity," a place that taught "truth" while maintaining the "spark of creativity that exists in all students."

This sounded great, so I went to work at daVinci. It wasn't for the money, which was never in excess, but because I liked that in our sometimes disorienting and dysfunctional world, there were still schools structured around the noble pursuit of truth.

I appreciated that this school's educational philosophy wasn't just a standardized formula handed down by Congress or textbook companies. Instead, daVinci cultivated a more organic human environment, one that embraced nontraditional students with blue hair or facial piercings and expected they could be just as — or more — brilliant than their more preppy, mainstream counterparts.

The school abandoned certain norms. There were, for example, no bells at the beginning or end of class. And teachers went by first names like the other normal humans one might run into at the grocery store or wave to while pumping gasoline.

Of course, where the school subtracted some norms, they also added their own practices—some of which were as unconventional as the students. For example, each week they hosted free schoolwide breakfasts of French toast and eggs for all students and staff. Although this breakfast buffet was nothing extraordinary on its own, when teachers sat with paper plates of scrambled eggs and listened to students talk about electric guitars and skateboards and anime, the definition of a teacher and what a teacher could be for a student got a little bit broader.

This was a subtle reminder that life was often improved by forgotten communal habits as simple as sitting down to eat and talk together. Or as simple as singing Happy Birthday out loud to students on their birthdays, which was something that Don—the seventy-one-year-old founding superintendent—did with some bravado for each and every student.

It was through these unconventional practices that one small school transcended rote academia to become a learning community.

But in this intended-to-be transcendent environment, I still sometimes remained firmly planted in the ground, sitting among my own inescapable dysfunction, completely disqualified to be a part of any sort of Eden.

Some days my patience with students was measured in ounces, not pounds, and cold Michigan mornings didn't stretch it further. Certain mornings I emerged from my bedroom like a mummy struggling out of the pyramid where I'd been buried for thousands of years. Groggy from lack of sleep or woozy-headed from a stubborn cold, I groped for caffeine and a hot shower. Inevitably, Wrigley had somehow tracked mud on every inch of the living room, as if all night he'd been dreaming about new murals he just couldn't wait to paw-paint onto the canvas of our floors and furniture. Already late, I couldn't find the can opener and faced the prospect of beating open my can of soup come lunchtime.

These were the days when, despite my love for teaching, I wished that I was a white-collar worker lost in cubicle-land, someone with the sort of job that can be modified to only involve emailing and faxing and doing as many non-person-to-person activities as possible.

But teaching, of course, is entirely person-to-person — person-to-*people* to be more accurate. The one-to-twenty-five ratio explained exactly why I couldn't just check in and then check out, grading papers or developing lesson plans. If I did, the fourteen-year-olds who share my room might eventually release their energy by throwing desks out the window.

I did consider my options in case this happened. I was sure I could inspire my English students to write about such an experience, journaling about how it felt to let the desk careen to its death on the cement below, from a first- or third-person point of view or using personification to describe the desk's last thoughts.

Since allowing such exercises would probably fast-track me to being pink-slipped, I instead spent the seven-minute drive to school pleading with God for just a little more patience than I was born with.

My drive-to-work prayers are cut and dry. I thank God for the beauty in my life and pray for the well-being of my family and my closest friends. Then I try to get things straight with God — to own up to who I am and reflect on who I want to be. By the time I've finished, I feel like I'm pointed in the direction of good and hope and truth.

On good days, this lasts for at least half an hour.

The first few minutes after I finish praying are glorious. I am always able to drive quite politely no matter how much worse the other drivers are than I am. With saintly patience, I calmly wait for my turn at the occasional stop sign, never scowling or honking or even mumbling under my breath.

Sometimes I even wave at joggers.

When I get to school, I am still pleasant and, I hope, radiating a sense of possibility and inspiration — a twenty-eight-year-old

Captain-My-Captain in sensible heels. As I step down the hallway with a cheery word of greeting for each student I pass, I am only *slightly* put off when the students, who interpret my friendliness as an invitation to camp out in my classroom, follow me to my desk like mice behind the Pied Piper.

I remind myself that my students aren't purposefully disrupting my setup time, but simply desire to connect with another human being who affirms them. Some want to tell stories about their lost dog or crazed boyfriend or broken computer. Others just want to be in a bright, noisy room.

And so as I juggle my keys, books, and unopenable can of soup —and think longingly of the percolating coffeemaker in the staff lounge—I offer polite "ahhhs" and "uh-huhs" while frantically praying that my students will drift away so I can get things done.

Reality is often the best incentive to pray.

My reality is this: Within minutes, the thirty chairs in front of me will be filled with only minimally attentive and waveringly respectful teens. And my job is to do backflips all day to inspire them to learn and hopefully, while doing so, transfer some of God's goodness through the life I try to pass off as an example.

Their number increases slowly. Here come the strangely responsible kids who arrive thirty minutes early and enjoy tasks like cleaning white boards and wiping down desks. Next come the groups of kids who have already exchanged the latest gossip at their lockers, and each of whom has an opening declaration with which to enlighten me.

"It's hot in here," the first one observes, scowling at me as she walks by as if I have purposefully jacked up the heat to make her learning experience sweatier.

I suggest cracking a window.

Next I hear a dreadful "Ughhhh!" accompanied by a terrible face, the face you make when you find a mangled raccoon dead on the side of the road. *"What* is that *smell?"*

I identify the smell to be "Eau de Teen," a popular scent in our school.

I note that I can only be responsible for my own personal hygiene. I am not on hand to remind each student to apply deodorant before leaving home. Let's face it: my plug-in air freshener only goes so far.

"You have *got* to be kidding me," complains a newcomer. "The window is open back here. It is *freezing*." She reports this as if Eskimos have just asked her to sit down on a giant ice cube in an igloo classroom where her first assignment will be to count polar bears.

I move her seat away from the window.

"I don't want her sitting over *here*," the next kid interjects. "She *talks* too much."

I refrain from saying that his complaint is one I could apply to most of my class.

And this is how my morning peace begins to fade, my resolve to embody Eden somehow withering away before the first nonbell has even not-rung.

In the midst of the seat switching and paper passing and Kleenex fetching, my sense of goodness and purpose blasts out of my mind and up into space, millions of miles away from my classroom.

When first hour ends, or when lunch arrives, or when the caravans of cars and vans pick up kids at the end of the day, Eden often goes uncultivated in my classroom. Instead, I sleepwalk through my routines, consumed by the thousand taxing details that demand my attention throughout the day.

Back in my car, and then back at home, the day's few remaining hours usually pass quickly. I make a meal, or watch from the stands as my husband coaches basketball. Later, when my mind is practically nonfunctional, I flip through a magazine or watch a rare television program.

Then the lovely and long-awaited moment finally arrives: my head settles softly into the downy comfort of my pillow. For a split second, I am blissfully and wholly at rest.

And then it hits me.

A distant thought comes careening back from outer space, crash-landing in my conscience like an asteroid.

Awwww, man. I meant to be a really good and patient teacher today.

This is literally the first time since 8:05 a.m. that I remember my serious morning resolution.

I lie there, staring at the ceiling, appalled by my own spiritual amnesia and barely able to keep my eyes propped open long enough to be appropriately disgusted with myself.

I begin apologizing, profusely, to a God somewhere beyond the ceiling I stare at, expressing my sorrow that I am the type of sniveling, dim-witted human who forgets her most serious goals fifteen minutes after making them.

This is my nightly prayer, a prayer no less real than my morning prayer as I drive to the office. Tonight—like last night, and the night before—I am almost too sorrowful to summon sufficient hope to pray that tomorrow will be different.

What kind of God has the patience to listen to such repetitious drivel? My Eden is not turning out as I planned and even if it was, I would not allow my impatient self to be a teacher there.

My words trail off as sleep takes me.

PART VIII

Dandelions are fierce in more than name. As the jagged leaves grow outward, they push down the surrounding vegetation and kill nearby plants by blocking the sunlight. This is how they clear the path for themselves and so many of their friends to grow.

1

AFTER MONTHS OF PURGING—OF TOYING WITH ANY GIMMICK I thought might produce transformation—there were *some* results.

My shoes, for example, were more organized than they had ever been—sectioned off in orderly rows of dress shoes or athletic wear or sandals. And my grocery list, which had always been carelessly scribbled on the backs of envelopes, was now officially laminated.

However, my failure to sustain change for even one school day testified that my transformation did not always proceed exactly as I had planned. Many days I felt like a faulty airliner that fails to take off after accelerating down the runway and is thus forced to turn around and taxi back to the starting point again.

My one-step-forward-two-steps-back approach to personal growth was similar to my early attempts at gardening.

They were not always pretty.

In fact, I'm pretty sure that my first garden singlehandedly lowered the property value of every home in our neighborhood, as if the city had decided to locate a sewage treatment plant at the end of the block. Patiently—stubbornly, really—I turned each plant, no matter what its original color, an exact matching shade of dried-out, straw yellow. I don't like to brag, but I have to say it was by far the best straw-yellow garden on the block, the type that would easily secure the blue ribbon in any county fair's straw-yellow category.

My secret can be summarized in two basic steps:

1. Plant flowers.
2. Neglect flowers.

Not everyone understood or appreciated the genius behind my prized gardening techniques.

My neighbor, for instance — who was probably jealous because her garden bloomed every color of the rainbow — tried to sabotage my straw-yellow motif by leaving several healthy, blooming plants on my porch. But I saw through her sinister plan and, through careful neglect, I was able to coax all the non-straw-yellow color from these plants as well.

Truth be told, I'm not really cut out to be a gardener, quite unlike my grandmother, who gardened as if it was the closest she could get to kneeling in the soil of heaven. So once I moved back indoors where I couldn't see my garden, it was easy to assume that it was doing just fine turning straw-yellow all by itself.

It was sometimes easier to push it out of my mind and forget I'd ever tried to garden in the first place.

2

Eventually, some combination of desire and guilt and unspoken social pressure led me to make a second attempt at gardening.

I quickly found that just *shopping* for flowers is tricky, never mind trying to grow them. I pushed my cart through the aisles, choosing flowers not by the labels that marked them as "hardy" or "needs sun," but instead choosing flowers that were—more important—not pink.

Pink is my least favorite color. This fact does not make gardening easy, since either quite a few gardeners have a thing for pink or my local home improvement stores are primarily targeting the residents of Barbie houses.

I managed to make it home with a collection of white and red and blue and orange flowers, and I promised myself that if, by some faulty labeling, a pink flower sprung up among them, I'd give natural selection a helping hand.

For some reason, my garden plot wasn't stretched out before me in a smooth square of nutrient-rich soil. Instead, a disheveled thicket of sticks and leaves had taken up residence in my yard, almost as if a former owner left the skeletons of her now-dead garden to haunt future landscapers.

Because I am not an especially passionate gardener, I was not bothered by being forced to leave my flowers in their plastic pots for now—which I figured gave them a slightly longer life expectancy than if I had planted them immediately anyways.

I pulled on my gloves and began to clear the sticks and leaves, but about twenty sticks into it, I was bored and hot.

I considered calling my dad to see if he would still pay me a penny per stick, which was the going rate for brush collecting in my elementary school days. If he agreed, and I used the old break-the-sticks-into-small-pieces-to-multiply-my-wages trick, I'd be able to afford the second wave of nonpink flowers after this set joins their previously departed ancestors.

As I entered the second hour of clearing, I was forced to admit that my stick-removal expertise was sorely lacking. I carried big handfuls of leaves and dried stems across the lawn to my trash bag near the curb. As I walked, loose debris fell through my fingers, creating trash-trails that I had to retrace and clean two or three times more.

This, I realized as I paused to wipe my forehead, was not unlike my life.

Four hours of hand-carrying sticks and leaves later, I suddenly remembered that we had this newfangled gadget in our garage called a wheelbarrow.

I have a knack for finding the hardest possible route to accomplishing household chores.

Wrigley, as it turns out, is not a champion gardener either. Unlike that wishbone dog on TV who would no doubt plant rows of petunias next to its master, Wrigley's only gardening skill is sampling new plants as I install them.

One summer, he ate twenty-one Asiatic lilies.

Besides chomping my flowers, as if each new plant that hits the soil is the daily special, Wrigley was determined, on this particular day, to help me clean up. So as I tossed a stick onto my growing brush pile, he decided—for the first time *in his entire life*—he'd fetch the stick from the pile and return it to the garden. And of course this day, the one day I was trying to wrangle my yard into obedience, Wrigley wanted to fetch every stick I threw on the pile. This day, he was suddenly the amazing fetching dog, who should be scheduled for David Letterman.

Not to be outsmarted by my Jack Russell, I moved to the other side of the fence, to the front yard, where he couldn't access my stick piles. Unfortunately, once I was there, Wrigley stood at the fence and barked at me as if I were the UPS man or some other intruder, because apparently from his angle he didn't recognize me under the bill of my baseball hat. If he were Superman's dog, he'd probably bark at Clark Kent.

Finally, it was time to plant my flowers. My rows were not perfect, nor was I absolutely certain the sunlight was going to hit them just right, but after a few hours of work, I looked around and saw flourishing young plants in place of the dried-out straw-yellow ones, and I was strangely satisfied with my progress.

I decided that this twelve-by-two-foot strip of the world was a better place because I lived. I quickly snapped a digital photo in case the evidence shriveled within the first twenty-four hours.

After this, because of my new gardening high, I began this outlandish, unheard of practice of checking in on my plants. I started with glancing out the window now and then to make sure the deer weren't trying to nab them, and eventually I began checking on them first thing in the morning when I let the dog out.

My newfound fondness for my garden even made me decide to do something radical: I decided to weed.

I hurried off to the lawn and garden store and explained to the oldest associate, who seemed like she had been planting gardens since Abraham Lincoln was in office, that I had some flowers I'd like to protect from weeds.

"I'm looking for something strong. *Really* strong," I emphasized, sounding like a drug user desperate for her next fix.

She ran a hand through her graying black ringlets, eyeing me as if she was trying to decide whether to enable my obvious addiction.

"I'll give you some weed-killer to start with," she said finally, as she heaved a bag of what I hoped was magic soil onto my cart. "This stuff is powerful. It's for gardeners who want to go in for the kill. If you lay it down around the weeds, you'll choke them all out."

I smiled maliciously. This was what I wanted: weapons for my garden warfare. I wanted my weeds to die.

"But—" my garden guru pronounced the word with finality as she looked me square in the eye. She was about to tell me a hard truth that was difficult to swallow. "The weeds will come back, you understand."

I nodded again.

"You can't just put this down once a month and hope there will never be weeds when company arrives."

Has this woman been spying on me?

"You have to actually watch for them and pull them when they break through the surface before they get a hold of your plants. The people with the healthiest gardens weed their gardens every day."

I nodded, deciding not to ask how healthy a garden might be on a once-a-week or once-every-other-week plan.

The garden guru read my mind.

"If you're okay with a mediocre garden," she said, "once-in-a-while weeding will do."

I looked at the floor, with some measure of guilt, my silence admitting that a mediocre garden was actually just fine with me. In fact, any garden that features colors other than straw-yellow plants and sticks would have been a significant improvement.

But what I'm *not* okay with is a mediocre life.

And my lazy weeding is evident in life too.

* * *

AFTER A FEW YEARS AT DAVINCI, I CHANGED JOBS—SWITCHING employment the way some people hop churches, hoping to find one that better fits their needs. In my case, I was hoping for a schedule that more closely matched my husband's work hours and a workplace nearer to the gym and softball fields where he spent many afternoons coaching after school.

This is not to say I stopped teaching high-school students, but rather that I applied to teach in a different school district altogether. I have known about Jackson High ever since I moved to this area, as its spired tower rises above the building line of the downtown strip like some sort of castle installed just a block off the main drag. The building is ironically gothic in style, which means it is the type of building more common to places like Princeton and Oxford and Cambridge — places that, unlike Jackson, are not most well known for housing the state prison.

I've heard that Woodrow Wilson said that gothic architecture "pointed every man's imagination to the earliest traditions of learning in the English-speaking race"* — which is, I guess, the same idea the Jacksonians were going for when they built the school back in 1927.

My favorite shot of the building is on a postcard, where the front of the building — its most photogenic side — is lit up by streetlights against a royal blue night sky. Three stories of dark brick rise above the basement, faced with white limestone moldings and, in some places, leaded-glass windows. There are even battlements on the top, the type of cut-outs where archers might place their arrows to defend a castle in an attack.

The high school is not generally attacked though, unless you count rivalries between local schools where we fight off the Lumen Christi Titans and so forth.

Last year, we acquired a beautiful bronze statue of a Viking couple that stands in the middle of the Circle Drive. The couple is patterned after historical Vikings, which means they don't closely resemble the typical sports mascot with horns, leading students to claim that we mistakenly paid for a statue of two wizards. This is not entirely a stretch, I suppose, as wizards may better belong to a

* http://etcweb.princeton.edu/Campus/text_gothicroots.html.

castlelike structure like our building, while Vikings probably raided castles more than resided in them.

More than the building, I was drawn to Jackson High by its diverse student population. By default, it serves as something of a hub for Jackson's city and its history—two things I had cycling interest in since college. But another prominent feature that drew me to Jackson High was the prospect of working with my husband, Chuck, who is a business teacher on the second floor.

Granted, when one already lives in the same house with one's husband, it is good to consider whether an additional eight hours of daytime exposure to said husband is wise. In this case, however, "working with" is a loose term that didn't necessarily imply walking hand-in-hand through the halls. Rather, it infers only that we are both swallowed up by the same enormous building where our fraternization is limited to nodding at each other during fire drill evacuations and returning each other's mail when senders don't account for there being two Cunninghams.

The year I switched to Jackson High was also the year I went from twenty-nine to thirty years of age, the year in which I was sure youthful idealism would end and adulthood would come barreling down on me. And perhaps it *was* a marker of sorts, as it was also the year I lost the luxury of blowing around aimlessly because I found out I was pregnant with our first child. This infant, who is only referred to as "Cheerio" as I write this—because that was the only shape that could be made out of my earliest ultrasound—seems like another surefire sign that I should keep growing as a person. After all, a half-grown person cannot be expected to raise something as small as a Cheerio to health.

From childhood to adulthood, from working in churches to working in schools, I'm beginning to realize that I need to see each new stage this way—as an opportunity to grow and change. To let God wipe away things and renew me.

By the time I started in my new classroom in the fall, my garden guru had inspired me, as had the newly-growing nonpink flowers in my yard. I returned to my classroom with new, twofold resolve.

First, I decided that if I saw a thriving weed—a personal weakness that was choking my growth—I would set out to kill it. Mercilessly. On the spot.

And second, I would be vigilant in case that weed, or a new one, ever tried to resurface.

This was much easier said than done. I had only delivered instructions to my class for all of six minutes before the first weed reared its head.

I stood in front of the classroom, which is the best place to glean everyone's attention, especially if you are as fluent in teacher lingo as I am. I use a lot of "every eye up here" and "side conversations need to stop," but try to stay away from blinking lights or counting down from five since my students are fourteen and past the point of singing clean-up songs and learning about colors and shapes.

Momentarily, my instruction was a complete success. *I am an inspiring teacher who captures every student's focus*, I thought ... at least for the few seconds until I actually began speaking again.

Then I realized that my voice was merely a Pavlovian bell for the shaggy kid in the back row to put his head down on his desk and for another kid to begin drawing endless concentric circles on his shoe.

Undeterred, I rapped on their desks with my knuckles to jar them awake as I passed by, and I explained the project at hand, starting with how the day's assignment tied into our learning objectives.

Most freshmen care about learning objectives about as much as they care about keeping the contents of their lockers alphabetically organized.

A few minutes into my lecture, a student raised her hand, seemingly in rush to ask a pertinent question.

I love it when students participate, and I called on her immediately.

"Uh, yeah ... can I get a drink?"

Students often begin their comments with "uh ... yeah," as if they have momentarily forgotten what they would like to say and must stall for a second before retrieving it from their memory banks.

"No, right now is really not the best time to get a drink," I responded politely. "You can get a drink when I'm done explaining the assignment."

I continued my instructions.

Then a second student got up to sharpen his pencil, loudly, in an old-fashioned sharpener that immediately broke into two pieces when he touched it, pencil shavings and graphite dust flying everywhere.

I suggested, as kindly as I could manage, that he should not have been sharpening his pencil during instructions since this was just a little bit distracting to me and to his fellow students.

Several nearby students promptly asserted that they didn't mind the grind of the sharpener. One of them reported that he thought it was actually soothing.

"Well, I mind," I clarified.

The pencil-sharpening rebel returned to his desk but not, of course, before slapping a couple of high fives, which distributed dark streaks on people's hands and caused quite the defensive ruckus.

I am good at ignoring ruckuses.

I smiled brightly as I passed out a handout that detailed the requirements of the assignment, down to the specifics like what sort of font and what sort of citations must be used. I mentioned that essential information like due dates and length are highlighted ... and underlined ... and bulleted.

Then the pencil sharpener's hand went up.

Good. At least he is paying attention now.

"Can I go wash this off my hands? I've got pencil dust all over me."

"If you could just wait a couple of minutes and focus, I would really appreciate it," I said with a forced smile.

Another hand went up.

"Do you know what time the soccer game is after school?"

This was when I diverted from my instructions into an extemporaneous, but kind, lecture on common sense in the classroom. I visited such topics as appropriate times to speak, remain silent, get up, and remain seated.

Satisfied, I returned to the project at hand. I wrote key information on the board and projected a PowerPoint slide with the same details onto the screen. Finally, I passed around an example of the finished project—one from an "A" student from a previous year.

While I was talking, most of the students were nodding along, pretending to make careful notations about this or that on the notebooks in front of them, smiling agreeably as if they loved me and were inspired by me and could not wait to begin their assignment.

Every time I march through steps like these in my classroom, I am fooled by this seeming clarity: the apparently successful transfer of information from me to them. I often feel a momentary twinge of satisfaction that I *am* a good teacher. Maybe even a *great* teacher.

Then the hands go up.

"Should we write our names on the left or right side of the paper?" This would have been a good question if it weren't for the fact that every assignment I have given this year and every assignment I've ever given over the entire course of my career has always involved labeling the right side. And also if I hadn't just explained this orally, with a handout, with a PowerPoint, and with a visual example.

Another student wanted to know if they should use blue or black ink. I told them, jokingly, that only yellow ink was acceptable.

The sarcastic kids chuckled, while the others began frantically searching their backpacks for a yellow pen. One girl has one in her locker, she thinks. Another one may have to wait until he gets home to ask his mom to buy him one.

The final hands that went up triggered the weeds in my life, the ones with the pointed dent-de-lion leaves that I need to cut down.

"So,"—the student paused an excruciatingly long time as his complex question coalesced into a form he could articulate—" ... like, what exactly are we doing?"

You know that old saying about how there are no stupid questions? It's a total lie.

I took a deep breath, the kind of you've-got-to-be-kidding-me breath you need if you're about to swim across the ocean a second time, and I provided a gracious, positive recap of everything I just said, including making a couple pen marks on his handout for further reference.

Another hand went up.

"Yes?" I ask through clenched teeth.

"Um ... I don't get the assignment."

I inquired if he was listening during the last fifteen minutes, a period of time during which we had done nothing besides explaining the assignment.

"Well, I was listening," he replied, as if I was the one who should have been paying attention, "but I couldn't hear everything because I was trying to sharpen my pencil."

This was when I snapped like a Venus flytrap who feeds on pencils.

"If you didn't listen to the instructions the first time," I growled, "you're going to need to ask someone else."

Weeds are sprouting up over every inch of my insides.

But this was not all I said, nor was it all I thought. I made an intentional effort to confine my lecture to statements that wouldn't get me fired.

"Come on, guys," I began in the I'm-attempting-to-be-cool-about-this-and-level-with-you sort of way, which quickly tailed off into pure venting about listening skills.

I thought that the lecture was shaping up nicely, tough but balanced, right up until the point when another student hopped up to sharpen his pencil.

I can move like lightning in such situations. I sped across the room, tapping the pencil sharpener on the shoulder before he turned the crank even one rotation.

"This is the kind of thing I'm talking about!" My voice was now becoming nasal and pointed. I was, in that moment, reaching the apex on the annoying teacher scale, simultaneously channeling Ben Stein's "Anyone? Anyone?" from *Ferris Bueller's Day Off* and the "Wahhh, Wahhh, Wahhh" of Charlie Brown's teachers. But I couldn't stop.

"Life is not going to stop for you and repeat all the things you missed along the way. You have to learn to *pay attention!*"

This was not the most terrible or destructive thing to say to my students. The principle behind my words is, as far as life lessons go, pretty important. But my voice was laced with a few drops of acid, a temporary bitterness that's incongruent with who I want to be and the goodness I want to embody.

And my eyes—shooting invisible tranquilizer darts—did imply that I wouldn't mind if the student fell into a long and deep sleep right now. Or that I wouldn't mind if he went to work turning a crank in a pencil sharpening factory for the rest of his life.

It wasn't until a fragile, socially awkward student raised her hand and asked, seemingly fearfully, "Would it be okay if I sharpened my pencil now?" that I began to feel the weeds springing up in me and tried to kill them.

I stopped midsentence and called the previous pencil sharpeners up to the front of the room.

"Hey," I said, quite forced at first, "you know all that stuff I just said? That was important. Because I need you to pay better attention in class. I need you to wait until I am done giving instructions to get drinks or sharpen pencils or throw things away. But *how I said it*, with that tone of voice, is not cool. That's not who I want to be to you guys and I'm sorry."

The kids stared at me, stunned.

One just looked embarrassed for me and mumbled, "No big deal," before shuffling back to his desk.

"Well, uh, that's okay, I guess," the other said. Then he joked with a smirk, "But don't let it happen again."

"I'll try not to," I promised with a smile, not just because for once it's quiet while I'm talking, but because I think my apology has helped him feel a little less like a screw-up and a little more valued. The goodness God wants for him—for all of us—seems a little more intact. My classroom was blooming just a little more beautifully that day.

And my pride is, after all, a small thing to let go of for this sort of gain.

In fact, I feel so good about what happened that I vow to do the same thing every time I catch my pride resurfacing.

I will pick weeds every day.

This is not always easy, and I don't always get it right. Kids, after all, are observant and blunt people who do not hesitate to tell me what they are thinking, even when it is as menial as the fact that they do not like the fluffy mock-turtleneck sweater someone gave me for Christmas last year. So even if I promote good most days, they will still call me out if I fail in a moment of impatience and say or do things I'm not proud of.

But this is not all bad. When I publicly repent of my failures, it reinforces to myself, and to my students, that I joined this profession to love and inspire them and to embody Eden's goodness, and not to have nervous breakdowns over pencil sharpeners.

"This is not who I want to be," I find myself saying, more and more, when I drift off course.

And while it's hard to humble myself in front of a room full of fourteen-year-olds, I find that the benefits are endless. Self-effacement is a discipline. It is a garden stake that slowly but surely trains the shape of a growing plant.

Over time, I've started to sense my exasperation building *before* I get to the breaking point. I see the shoe-drawers and the sleepers and the pencil sharpeners bopping around like moles in an arcade game during my instructions. I feel my pride wanting to pound them on the head and back into their holes with a padded mallet.

Yet more and more often I learn not to pull the trigger, not to explode in a selfish release of my frustrations. Instead, I choose to do more constructive things. I have quiet, firm conversations with kids who are off-task, and I try to treat them as people who, with a little hard work, have potential for great success. Over time, these measured responses become more ordinary than the others. They begin to become the default, the things I want to do out of habit and new instinct and not just out of discipline.

In such moments I am amazed at the simplicity of change, hiding beneath all the layers I allow to grow up around it.

PART IX

Most gardeners consider the dandelion the enemy, a fraudulent and cheap flower that tries to crash their landscapes without an invitation. But a gardener who loves a small child—a child who regards dandelions with naïve delight—might allow a few inches of space for this errant, yellow, tufted plant.

After all, the Master Gardener knows how to work even the most flawed plants into his beautiful landscapes. He is one of the only beings, perhaps, who, when choosing plants for his masterpieces, could get away with picking weeds.

1

I ADMIT, I HAVE FLIRTED WITH CHANGE THE SAME WAY I HAVE FLIRTED with gardening.

What I lacked in both cases was not just experience, but any sort of direction as to how to lay out my garden—or my life—to promote growth. I found, for example, that even with regular weeding, some plants could not thrive where I had placed—or rather, misplaced—them. They did not have enough sun or shade or perhaps they didn't belong in Michigan at all.

A hundred and one dead plants in, I realized that if I wanted to sustain my garden's growth over the long term, I would also need to familiarize myself with gardening principles. Perhaps browse some "gardening layouts"—tools that help a gardener position plants in the locations where they will thrive.

Direction, of course, is what I lacked in life too. I had been faithfully weeding for a while, attacking my flaws left and right, knowing that they must die, but I had no idea how to grow a healthier, fuller life in the extra space I was creating.

I needed a blueprint, the layout of a master.

2

As a child, I gave my life to God one night in a prayer, handing it over freely, as if I were extending him a dandelion. This was an instinctive gesture on my part—to share myself, to make God smile—rather than the sort of philosophical shift that one might imagine of a spiritual conversion.

I wasn't aware my prayer would be considered a conversion at all or that, as a result, I would be added to world databases of religious adherents under the category of Christianity. I didn't even know such a category existed. I had no thought of Brethrens or Baptists or Methodists or nondenominationals, but only a childlike preference to follow Jesus over the status quo, in a way that—at the time—seemed only a little more serious than my preference for strawberry jelly over grape or Rainbow Brite over She-Ra.

As I began exploring God, browsing faith the way kids rummage about their backyard, amazed by anthills and Monarch butterflies and moss-covered rocks, society got busy inducting me into the systems it had built to process religious events. For instance, what had once been a simple prayer—the expression of a childish impulse to believe in God—was later marked as the beginning and end of my "religious conversion." The singular event was written onto the calendar in one specific box and into the front page of my Bible, like birth certificates to formally recognize the day that I began my reborn life.

The day, of course, though a spiritual mile marker, became more of a pleasant memory from my childhood, one that—as time passed—I remembered with little more detail than I retained about the day of my own physical birth. My conversion became one of those events that sounded vaguely familiar as adults who were there describe them. Do you remember when you got stung by a bee and you ran wailing down the center aisle of the church while your dad was preaching? Do you remember hurling yourself out of your crib onto your head to escape your nighttime sleeping arrangements? Do you remember that one night, before you fell asleep, when you announced you wanted to ask Jesus into your heart?

Although my initial prayer was all sincerity and heart, over time I internalized my conversion the way it seemed like one was supposed to. The day I asked Jesus into my heart was over and done with, locked into the past along with the day I went on a field trip to the zoo or the day David swallowed a matchbox wheel and had to go to the hospital.

And so faith started and completed itself all in one night in a Winnie-the-Pooh wallpapered bedroom while a wooden swing hung from hooks in the ceiling. And for many years to come, I think, it stayed in that room, swinging among the stuffed animals, instead of growing up and moving on with me when I moved out into the land of adulthood.

This is why I eventually needed a new metaphor to describe my ongoing choice to follow after God beyond the days of one- and three-dunk baptisms, lobbying for brown church shingles, and reorganizing my closet in the name of God.

Ironically, I found the new metaphor for ongoing transformation in the last days I spent with my maternal grandmother, who was perhaps best known for being a gardener.

3

MARION LUCY BAKER WAS A RELENTLESS AND BOISTEROUS BRIT WHO, despite her sixty years in the States, never entirely lost her accent. Solid English words like "davenport" and "pocket book" fortified her vocabulary, and she never wasted the opportunity to use her favorite British terms — or any words, for that matter.

This was a dominant gene, I'm afraid.

It was not just words that Marion Lucy had in excess; she also dished out her opinions the same way she served apple pie — you were given another helping whether you asked for it or not.

Again, a dominant gene.

My first memories of Nana, as we called her, appear in mental video clips of my grandparents "arguing." This was back when Poppa was quiet simply because he *was quiet* and not quiet because he had suffered a stroke.

"Sit down, old lady!" Poppa would finally break from his silence to say to Nana, as she raced laps around the kitchen baking four kinds of pies to suit the four different tastes of her Thanksgiving dinner guests.

"I will sit down when I am ready to sit down, old man!" Nana would bark back.

And we, the grandchildren, racing matchbox cars on the practical berber carpet, stifled giggles — thinking their interchange was funny, but not funny enough to risk laughing out loud and incurring a tongue-lashing from Nana.

Nana never seemed short on steam. Although my brothers and I weren't around to witness the Marion Lucy of the 1940s, plenty of stories survived to paint a vivid picture.

Nana told us piles of deliciously stubborn stories, drawn from ordinary daily affairs like administering medicine to the family poodles. One poodle—paradoxically named Angel—was particularly close-lipped, and it fell to Marion Lucy to convince the delinquent canine to swallow just one spoonful of syrupy medicine per day.

According to Poppa's seldom-heard version, Nana and Angel were almost equally stubborn in their face-off, which is like saying that the stone statuette in their garden was *almost* as big as Mount Rushmore.

The poodle never stood a chance.

Poppa had the audacity to offer Nana a few suggestions for coaxing Angel into taking a spoonful of the veterinarian's liquid brew.

"I told your grandfather in no uncertain terms," recalled Nana, mimicking the sternness of her younger self, "that if he said one more word—*one more word*—I would shove the spoonful of dog's medicine right down his throat."

Unfortunately, Poppa continued sputtering, "But . . . but . . ." and that was enough for Marion Lucy. She pushed the spoon into Poppa's partially open mouth, as he looked on stunned at the unapologetic guts of his feisty, British war bride.

Of course, Poppa had his own silent strength and it was not long until he had his quiet revenge. Not much later, he stood methodically painting the fence that he built himself. As he painted the gate posts, Marion Lucy walked over and began telling him, in her thick British accent, just how he ought to be painting.

Poppa said nothing.

His only response was the serene drip, drip, drip of a paint brush, which spotted her dark tresses with bright globs for a full ten seconds before she caught on.

At this point in the story, they always laughed. American soldier and British bride. Her voluminous sing-songy pitch and his soft chuckle harmonized at the story's climax, a soundtrack playing for the millionth time.

Nana's strong will shouldn't have surprised my young grandfather. After all, Marion Lucy had been tenacious from the beginning.

The two of them met in her native Britain where Poppa was stationed during World War II. She was serving as a telephone operator and made no secret that she had employed her trademark spunk to disconnect calls from other British lasses to my grandfather.

Poppa never stood a chance either.

At just nineteen years old, Marion Lucy left everything she knew and loved to marry Poppa and come to America. This part of their story astounds me. Admittedly, Poppa was a catch. A civil servant and model citizen, and not bad to look at, given the black-and-white photos of the much younger him in uniform. Yet I can't imagine what series of miracles would have had to occur for me to even consider, at nineteen years old, leaving my homeland, my family, my friends.

And so, perhaps in order to survive, Marion Lucy learned to wear her tenacity on her sleeve, right beside her heart. This, and a faith nurtured in the stone church of the old English manor where she spent her childhood, allowed her to not only survive a move across the Atlantic, but to do it so successfully that she was still happily married to the same American soldier when my husband and I wed on their anniversary fifty-seven years later.

I sometimes finger Marion Lucy's original gold wedding band that hangs around my neck and remember that my life is a tangible fruit of two people's decades-long devotion.

On Nana's deathbed, which was not a single event but a long stretch of deathbed moments, she talked more frequently about the old days. Although I had heard the stories before, they took on particular importance, as it was apparent these would likely be some of the last times I would hear them in her own feisty vernacular.

Nana's voice, still unashamedly British though strained from cancer meds and broken up by coughs, recounted the tales all over again—starting with her initial boat trip across the ocean when she stared out into the expansive abyss of dark Atlantic waters. Her face grew somber as she remembered gazing over the ship's railing. It was here, Marion Lucy reported, "that I realized for the first time what I had done."

The last hours of the voyage were particularly long, Marion Lucy recalled, full of bits of regrets and sadness over what had been left on increasingly distant British shores and, at the same time, marked with anxiety and anticipation at what lay ahead in rebellious, revolutionary, legendary America.

I gaped with her, feeling the same thud in my stomach, as I imagined the thousands of miles of separation setting in.

"When the boat reached the harbor and I could make out a gray-colored shoreline in the horizon, my heart sank with the fear of living in a strange land," Nana told me. I see her in my mind's eye, like a character in a movie, in her sturdy green skirt and practical blazer, her hat tipped slightly to one side, staring glassy-eyed into the distance. Fear bubbles beneath her bravery.

"But just as tears started to well up in my eyes," Nana recounted, "I heard a thunderous cheer from the deck below. And what do you think it was, but all of the servicemen whooping and hollering to be back home after their tour overseas. And I did not know exactly what it was that had inspired them, all at once, to let out a cheer ... until I looked up, through my tears, to see the boat approaching Lady Liberty—the Statue of Liberty, with her torch raised as if to greet us all and welcome us to the United States. The servicemen's victorious shouting was in anticipation of kissing the ground of home sweet home after defeating madman Hitler in the war. After that, I could not shed a single tear."

Marion Lucy smiled after sharing the story, a peaceful smile, a smile I know well from her own brown eyes and slightly crooked smile and from my own. It means, *no matter, no matter, all is well.*

And for all the talk of France giving the Statue of Liberty to be a symbol of hope and encouragement for the huddled masses, Marion

Lucy said, Lady Liberty was just that. However, once on shore at New York's Ellis Island, the process of becoming an American citizen wasn't as hopeful as the gleaming green queen of the Big Apple had led her to believe.

Nana reported that the classes for prospective citizens were sheer misery. But there was only one way to move—forward—because, as she paused to note, "It was not so simple as it is today to get on a plane and head back to Europe."

"What I remember most of all is that this man"—she says "this man" as if she wants to break proper British behavior and spit, her face full of disgust—"who worked for the state lined us all up. All of us who had come in from other countries. There were Germans and Swedes and other Brits. And he asked each of us a question." Her voice is tense.

"The immigration man wanted to know whether we would swear, in that moment, to take up arms against our home countries." She turns to me, and translates, just in case I haven't understood. "He wanted to know if I would fight against England, against my father and mother, against my brother, should our countries ever find themselves at war."

Marion Lucy paused here, astounded, as if this stern immigration official just asked her this question for the first time five minutes ago.

She turned to me, incredulously, as if I were a fellow immigrant who would share her outrage at being asked to make such a choice. "Can you believe it?!"

I shook my head no, which was the only appropriate thing to do. I learned early on that when Marion Lucy asks a rhetorical question, you answer in whatever way aligns with her intention in asking it. It wouldn't have surprised me if her cancer-ridden body still had it in her to leap out of its bed and strangle some sense into me if necessary.

"Several people walked right off the line," she told me, and then she adds defiantly, "and I didn't blame them."

She paused again, summoning a fifty-year-old emotional response inspired by being asked to switch her loyalty from one country to another.

"What did you do?" I asked, sincere suspense somehow filling my voice despite having heard the story dozens of times before. This would be Nana's last time telling me the story, and it was the first time that I *needed* her answer to speak possibility into my own life.

I needed to declare my own allegiance, to align myself with a new ruler, to embrace an entirely new set of ideals. I was leaving the far country and returning to my Father, hat in hand. I was ready, whatever the cost, to begin something new.

"What did you do?" I repeated.

Nana looked at me.

"I did the only thing I could."

Some changes come upon you with such suddenness, such intensity, that you do the only thing you can do. You hold your breath and let the wave carry you to a new shore.

She continued, "I asked myself over and over again, 'Could I *really* take up arms against my own country?'"

I wondered with her. Could I? Could I turn my back on society's norms? Could I drop bombs on my perfectly socialized, middle-class, American-dream, rat-race materialism?

"I decided that if this was going to be my life, and my husband was going to be here in America, and if America was going to be home to my future children, that I could take up arms against anyone—even my own people—to defend my new life and family. Because I believed the future would be worth it."

Nana then turned to me and told me that it was worth it.

"The future is worth it. I'm sure of it." She smiled at me, and I knew that for her, I was a part of the future that made the voyage worth it. "Wouldn't trade it for the world."

I sat beside my grandmother that day in a black leather-bound rocking chair that dates back to Civil War times, looking at ovular Victorian-framed black-and-white photos of ancestors I'll never know. Marion Lucy Stowe—my oldest living maternal relative—was telling me how she began life all over again, how she was reborn as an American citizen.

It started with a single conversion moment when she stood at an altar, her long, smooth fingers folded into my grandfather's, and said, "I do." But even at that moment, Marion Lucy could not have anticipated all the things that she would have to learn and internalize over her lifetime to fully embrace a new way of life. Slowly, patiently, she had to experience America for herself, to learn the history of her new country, participate in its rituals, and make sense of its language.

Like the dandelion, she had to be broken, separated from her motherland and from family and friends to be planted on a new shore. And once in America, Marion Lucy hit some walls and she also had to do some weeding just like me. She had to abandon old habits— British ways of doing things—that were incompatible with her new country.

"Your aunt was not too happy with me when she brought home her report card," Nana remembered. "I had taught her all the British spellings—c-o-l-o-u-r and t-h-e-a-t-r-e and another half dozen words like that—which of course seemed perfectly correct to me, but failed to impress her spelling teacher."

"And for months, I thought your great grandmother was a fibber," she admitted with a laugh. "Every Saturday when we prepared to clean the house, she would announce 'we're gonna go to town!' But when the work was done, she always backed out on her promise. We *never* went to town. Much later, someone finally explained to me that Americans in that time period said 'go to town' when they meant they wanted to really do the job well."

Nana paused and I could almost see her mind rewinding through history. "There were so many, many changes I had to make."

But after many years of living in America and all the routine changes—big and small—my grandmother emerged as American as anyone else. And this is where I found my new metaphor. A metaphor that speaks of faith not just in terms of a single day of rebirth, of agreeing to give over one's life, but of faith that grows like one's allegiance to a new country.

The story of my grandmother's life was an odd place to find language to describe my faith journey, but it's where I found it just the same. As I pondered her naturalization to the United States, my own spiritual role began to make sense as well. I had landed at the port of God's kingdom early in life, early enough that I could barely remember life before I reached this destination. And I had given my life to God, then, before I really understood all it meant to do so.

But now, I was beginning to understand. Like the young Marion Lucy in a new country, I still needed to learn more about my country and king, to align myself to his vision and to pledge my allegiance with each year of adulthood.

4

My grandmother arrived in the United States long after the founding fathers debated our nation's ideals in great halls and long after Revolutionary soldiers took up arms to fight for them. As a result, she never got to see the fiery passion of James Madison as he championed his convictions. She never heard the wise resolve of Thomas Jefferson as he contemplated a better way of life than the settlers had known back in England.

Instead, of course, Nana had to rely on the documents these men wrote—the Constitution and the Declaration of Independence—along with what historians said about them, in order to piece together who they were and what their country stood for. And although my grandmother was a bright woman who would've made careful observations about even the driest of history books, the words—out of context—may not have moved her as those men intended.

It is not that Nana was incapable of grasping intellectual ideas, because she was, but rather she was missing a valuable component. She was not able to see the raw emotion of these two frustrated visionaries, or to share in the camaraderie between them, or to witness the inspiration that leaked from them to young farmers who would lay down their lives for the new country the pair of men envisioned. The human elements—the feelings, gestures, expressions, exchanges—could not be fully transferred by even the most comprehensive historian.

My grandmother's struggle would not have been completely unlike mine, then, born long after Christ and even longer after Eden, but trying desperately to sense the spirit behind the written documents and history of Christian tradition that present God and his intentions to the world today.

For this reason, I have been both frustrated and moved while reading portions of the Bible—the Ten Commandments or the Sermon on the Mount—the laws and speeches that constituted God's kingdom. I am forced to grapple with printed words on a page, without the ability to see Jesus Christ stand on a hillside, in all his humanness and all his God-ness, passionately advocating for a better way of life than the one most people are experiencing.

Admittedly, the words on a page sometimes lack context and energy—either because my rational mind dilutes them to boring historical record or because my emotional boredom saps them of meaning after hearing them referenced to seeming monotony.

And I think, *This is not how I want to read this.*

Like the people who traveled cross-country to see Martin Luther King Jr. or Abraham Lincoln in person, I wish I could travel across time to stand in the same era as Jesus. Can you imagine—pressing into the crowd, pushing up on your tiptoes, trying to get a good angle, trying to see Jesus' face? Listening with anticipation, tracking with him from one idea to the next, drawing immediate connections between his message and our lives? And slowly, I suspect, his ideas would grab us and we would find ourselves owning his vision, thinking to ourselves, *yes, that's it, that's the way to live.*

And before it was all over, in a display of allegiance that surprised even ourselves, we'd be clapping our hands together in wild agreement and maybe even climbing up on our chairs to yell uncharacteristic applause. And when word traveled through the countryside that thousands of people had gathered to hear some revolutionary named Jesus, we could say, "We were there." We could say, "We are part of that movement."

On one of the days I found myself wishing this, I packed my trademark iced tea and my favorite fuzzy orange blanket and my adobe-colored Bible into a mesh beach bag and drove the mile stretch between our house and a local park, which happens to be the location of the nearest grassy hillside. I climbed up on one hill, high enough that I could've addressed the public meandering about the park below, and I read Matthew 5, Jesus' State of the Union Address, the garden layout of the kingdom God had intended since Eden.

I sat cross-legged, the eager listener, as if I was leaning forward into my Bible, waiting to hear the rich vision of a philosopher and intellectual, a revolutionary and a personal friend. And then I began reading Jesus' vision — a vision of a society where people did not judge each other, where people kept their word, where citizens regularly went the extra mile for their neighbors.

I tried to imagine the emotional response rising in the crowd that would've listened to him. A lady, marginalized by society, who had a habit of keeping her face lowered to the ground, glancing up in cautious agreement when Jesus said "do not judge." An ex-servant who grins from ear to ear, barely able to keep from jumping up and down when Jesus says, "Let your yes be yes," because his master recently did just this and released him from indentured service as promised. Two neighbors, who walked a long distance to the hillside together, who had raised children together, assisted each other in times of hardship, sharing a knowing smile over their history of going the extra mile for each other.

In his kingdom, Jesus said, people would not only live in peace with their neighbors, but they would show love to their enemies and even pray for those who harassed them. In his kingdom, Jesus said, people would quietly do good instead of crowing about their accomplishments. In his kingdom, Jesus said, citizens wouldn't need to worry because it would be abundantly clear that this king never stopped providing for his people.

I tried to imagine how my heart would've beat a little faster with each line. *Who wouldn't want to live in a place where the people operated like this?*

I imagined what I would be doing had I been there; how those words would make me feel. Maybe I would've been trying to memorize the things he was saying so I could relay these ideals to other people back home. Or I might've tried to catch his eye just to nod at him in affirmation. *I get you. I get it. We're on the same page. I want the life you're describing.*

I suspect I would've tried to edge my way to the front, so I could see Jesus closer, catch the expressions on his face, the movements of his hand, the flicker in his eyes. I'd take in his followers—Who were they? Where were they from? How long had they been following? *Can I come? I'd be willing to throw in on this. Seriously. I believe in what you're talking about.*

When I finished reading, a prayer had begun forming—less in gracious "Our Father" fashion and more in a tumble of words borrowed from national anthems and Constitutions and pieces of Sunday school classes and Dad's Sunday sermons.

I imagined myself entering an expansive hall with high ceilings and marble columns leading to a single throne, set on a platform, above eye level—an image mashed together from movies like *Three Musketeers* and *Lord of the Rings*. There, in the palace, I waited behind rows of other supplicants for my chance to be in the presence of the king. And when it was finally my turn, I pictured myself on one knee, bowing my head to present myself a loyal subject. A sort of pledge of allegiance spilled out then, not necessarily the kind that rises in words, but that swells in the emotions of a soldier's heart when he locks eyes with his leader on the front lines of the battlefield.

After a reverent pause, I lifted my eyes to meet the king's so he could see the seriousness of my promise. *What can I do for you, my Lord? I will do anything you ask of me.*

And I knew when I said this that the offer held both promise and danger—as one day a king might need his follower to raise a toast to a fruitful year and on another he might need someone to lead a charge into bullets on the front line of battle. One day life might allow you to blow about, carefree, and another might send you crashing into a wall.

But I knew that this was the way it worked. And so I nodded in acceptance, letting the king know I understood what the journey would entail.

And instead of ending with the traditional "amen," I looked at the ruler on the throne — the same man who had stood on a hillside and cast a vision for a new way of life, the Son of the same God who had made Eden good — and concluded with one simple line.

I serve at the pleasure of the King.

The details of the kingdom as laid out in the Sermon on the Mount and the other books of the Bible became the garden layout I had been looking for. They were the master guidelines that outlined where to remain planted, how to source myself, and how to grow. And I knew as I practiced these things I would not be changed in only one conversion moment, but rather I would change like my grandmother did when she came to this country. Gradually, as I slowly weeded out old ways and adopted new ones, I would be naturalized to a new way of life and begin to understand my role as a subject of the king.

5

OVER TIME I FELT MORE COMFORTABLE IN MY PRAYERS, SENSING THAT the king embraced me, not as an unfamiliar subject, but with the welcome he might extend toward his child.

"Come closer, Sarah," he would say. "You must get to know me well, daughter. To press into my kingdom and embrace everything I have to teach you. Because I want you to walk the open streets of life, to shake hands and kiss babies and to love on people, as a representative of my Eden."

This gradually began to make sense to me. After all, I had long understood what it meant to be part of a hope-bearing family.

For as long as I could remember, families in our community had called upon spiritual leaders like my father to come to their sides after accidents or near-death illnesses. And I had seen, in such moments, that when people like my pastor-father walked in, he offered those who looked to him a little piece of comfort, the hope and solidity of the timeless God he served.

But the older I got, the more I also understood that if an emergency call came into our family's home while my father was away, my brothers—David and John—and I could go to the hospital in my father's place. And in that same hospital, that same family's eyes would fall upon us, the pastor's three children, and we would represent to them at least a fraction of what our father did. In those moments, we would carry with us the same sort of peace and hope, light and life, that he taught us to embrace and embody.

In this same way, I sensed, I could walk life's streets, bearing the hope of God himself.

6

As I work toward experiencing and embodying Eden, I can't help but remember the last days of my grandmother Marion Lucy.

I spent a week at my grandmother's house, helping her weed out her life.

Nearing eighty at the time, my grandmother could look at most of the possessions she had acquired in life and say with some frankness that she would not need them again.

Camping equipment, for example, was tossed without a second thought.

However, Nana was not equally willing to part with *everything*. She was still quite attached to a fourteen-pound bowling ball with her name inscribed on it. She handed it to me, with some difficulty. "Now, I'm going to give this to you," she said, and then added, quite seriously, "but I want you to hold onto it in case I want it back."

Occasionally, as we sorted through her possessions, Nana would make rare comments critiquing her life. "I don't know where I got all this stuff," she'd say. "I could've been more generous. I could've done more."

This was always hard to hear, as Nana and Poppa were well known for their generosity. They would be among the last on the planet to be critiqued as miserly. But watching my grandmother weed out her life was a memorable reminder to me that in the end, I will wish I had weeded more, not less.

7

LAST MEMORIAL DAY, THE YEAR AFTER BOTH MY GRANDMOTHER AND grandfather died, my family and our spouses traveled to my Poppa's home to spend a few days in the magical backyard garden Nana had created in her life.

The garden, however, now a year after her passing and a couple years since she was able to work in it regularly, was a painful sight. It was overgrown and tangled, grandfather trees tangled up in umbrella trees and ivy stitching everything together into a jungle that we had to hack through with gardening shears. Some parts were overcrowded, strangling each other, forcing us to pick lawn bags full of weeds until the front yard could hold no more. We removed plants that were growing too close together, threatening their neighbors. And we plucked out a few flowers here and there to take home in pots to our own gardens where they would bloom again in the spring.

In this context, sandwiched between death and life, it was unquestionable that bad things had to be chopped out, removed, or killed—not for the sake of external visual appeal or affirmation, but because some things have to die so that others can live.

This is when I realized the secret my garden-loving grandmother shared with God all along: Picking weeds is a beautiful thing.

ACKNOWLEDGMENTS

I AM STILL A DEEPLY FLAWED HUMAN BEING WHO HAS A LOT OF changes left to make. But my life would be even more flawed if the following people had left me to figure it out on my own:

My infant son, Justus, who was born as this book was being edited, began changing my life while still in the womb. I suspect this is only the beginning.

My husband, Chuck, who has handled change beautifully, recently shifted from being an avid sports addict to being a slightly *less* avid sports addict, so he has time and energy for being such a devoted father.

My dad, Harold Raymond, currently fifty-eight, who recently changed his life by planting another church as he nears the age most people retire. Perhaps this courage comes from his dad, Tom Raymond, who in his mid-eighties shocked us all by leaving his lifelong home city of Columbus, Ohio, and buying a house out in the country in Michigan, where he attends my dad's new church.

Denny West, who changed his life around several times to serve as an elder in three of my dad's churches, including the recent plant, before eventually succumbing to cancer and joining God in eternity in 2009. Rose Hunt, whose life and death inspired hundreds of Summerfield community members to return home for a 5K fundraiser in her honor (*theroserun.com*).

My family, including the addition of my beautiful niece, Grace, whose birth in 2008 convinced me that babies are worth the life change. And my new sister-in-law, Jill Bailey Raymond, who changed me from being an eight-months pregnant woman to an eight-months pregnant bridesmaid.

Jennie Timmons, who changed her life by marrying Randy Sottovia on July 11, 2009. And to Bethany Timmons, who just bought her first house.

My cohorts from Concordia University's class of 2009, especially Aaron and Aleta who at times carried me on their backs through all the changes as we worked to finish our master's degrees together.

The people who made the places mentioned in this book significant. Thanks to New Life, Summerfield, Spring Arbor, Olive Branch, Lawndale, Westwinds, daVinci, Dr. Cassitty's office, and the relief workers and volunteers of Ground Zero, especially John Desimone and his partner, Danny.

Erik, Jessica, Hastings, Zessin, Joe, Lori, Mike, Monica, Lindsey, Jack, Libby, Sheryl, Willard, Lisa, Christy, Andrea, Laura, Kelly, Nate, Jen, Beth, and the other staff of Jackson High School, especially the Business and English departments, the Friday Hunt Club crew, and the frequenters of the second-floor lounge.

Dr. Vendola and his staff, Dr. Scott, Bobbi, and the labor-and-delivery staff at Allegiance Hospital, who navigated the changes in my pregnancy to make sure Justus got to us safely.

The staff at Zondervan, who have allowed my writing to change with my life.

God, who began a good work in me and will be faithful to complete it (Philippians 1:6).

Dear Church

Letters from a Disillusioned Generation

Sarah Cunningham

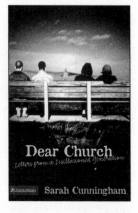

Dear Church is a series of letters from a twenty-something to the global church she's not always sure she wants to be a part of. The author's story awakens the voice of a younger generation whose attendance in the church is dropping, yet she encourages the church that their Christian faith is still alive and well. In the end, *Dear Church* tells a story that will be familiar to every age group: the story of overcoming disillusionment and staying the course.

Softcover: 978-0-310-26958-8